ACES AND KINGS

No. 1 SQUADRON, AUSTRALIAN FLYING CORPS

In foreground: Major Williams, D.S.O., with cane.   Canine escort: "Mick" and "Charlie."

ACES AND KINGS

By

L. W. SUTHERLAND, M.C., D.C.M.

Written in collaboration with
NORMAN ELLISON

PUBLISHERS
JOHN HAMILTON
LONDON

FOREWORD

The Great War has fallen back into the past, very far back as many of its soldier survivors feel; and yet, if it should have been supposed that all its stories of gallantry and romance have been told, books like this of Flight-Lieutenant Sutherland's still appear to disprove the presumption and to delight all lovers of adventure. The author was an officer in No. 1 Squadron of the Australian Flying Corps, which operated in a Royal Flying Corps wing in support of Allenby's great campaign in Palestine. The Australian No. 1 Squadron became the most redoubtable unit in that aerial arm. Its performances are a well-known story. This book aims rather at revealing the human stuff that went to make it; and its tales of the lighter side of an exacting service will delight every reader. To this present writer, whose researches for the compiling of the official history of the Australian Flying Corps brought him into happy acquaintance with many of its pilots, to be asked to introduce the author of these reminiscences to his public is a high compliment; but that public will hardly require any encomium of a book whose merits speak so plainly for themselves.

The Palestine campaign, the Last Crusade, can never be divorced from romance, although the tribulations of the desert, added to the exhaustion of the fighting and the labour on the lines of communication necessary to support it, often obscured that romance from the troops engaged. Yet it illumines the whole story in retrospect. The release to a wider public of Lawrence's magnificent narrative has revealed one side of the adventure; but the chronicles of the Australian Light Horse and the airmen in the smaller desert of Sinai, and in the world-old war-theatre of Palestine, offer, as they are unfolded, adventure no less entrancing, especially to their own countrymen. These airmen even made friends of the German airmen they continued to fight. It is a great loss that Ross Smith did not live to write his own account of a splendid company in which he was, by general acknowledgment, king. It would seem, too, that so many of these great-hearted fellows lacked the facility, or the initiative, to write that " inside story " which they have relied upon history (visualized as some sort of all-seeing intelligence) to recover by superhuman means of its own. How far history is apt to fall short of recording the vital, human side of the narrative may be perceived from these instances of the sort of alleviations that made endurance of the war possible, and so its history, as recorded, to be enacted.

Not least is the author to be congratulated on the happiness of the title he has chosen.

Sydney.   F. M. CUTLACK.

CONTENTS

ILLUSTRATIONS

CHAPTER I

If you were not " over there," and if someone who knows has not told you, my stories may give you a wrong impression of aerial warfare. These yarns are true. But, reading them over, it strikes me that the idea may be created that it was only the pilots and the observers who did things ; who really counted. Not at all. The best pilot, the prince of observers, would not have been worth a burial service unless he had had the right kind of backing on the ground. None knew this better than the " Higher-ups." Still, during the war, it was only the pilot whose name got into the *communiqués*, who received the bouquets in the newspapers. Of course, considerations of public morale had a lot to do with this : it bucked the " civvies " up to know that a Bishop, a McCudden, or a Mannock was writing lengthy individual casualty lists among the opposition war-birds. And, after all, surnames were more tangible than foreign geographical names—it was probably more heartening to the folk back home to learn that one of our aces had shot down three more Huns than that we had advanced 200 yards on a mile front at some unpronounceable place of which they had never previously heard.

But I am wandering. What I wanted to say, and what I hope to be able to prove to you, is that the pilot was, after all, only one of a team ; that there were many other chaps playing, and that all earned their " places." Come for a ramble with me round our squadron and let me introduce you.

Here, in three E.P. (Egyptian Pattern) tents, is the administrative H.Q. The C.O. has one ; he is too busy to be disturbed. The Recording Officer has another. You are probably not interested in statistics, and maps, and official reports. Right, we can give that tent a miss too. And, of course, you do not want to see the orderly room. No one could blame you for that. Oh, yes, I have had some unpleasant interviews there. But that's my secret. If you ask painful questions, you will have to get another guide.

These three Bessenau hangars house the machines, one flight to each—" A," " B," and " C." " C " Flight is nearest. Pop in—we'll see the men at work. Yes, the hangar looks flimsy ; it's only a canvas cover over timber. It has to be easily transportable. But it will be serviceable for quite a long time, if proper care is taken of the covering. Wind is the worst trouble. The hangar comfortably holds six Bristols ; that is the strength of " C " Flight. Where are the six ? Well, two of them are out on " reco "; two in the hangar; and those two out there on the tarmac are " standing by " for a Hostile Aircraft alarm. The two men in attendance on each machine are the engine-man and the rigger. When the alarm sounds, their job is to start the engines immediately. You can see the flying-kits of the pilots and observers hanging over their cockpits. Yes, it is something like in a fire brigade station—the same air of alert preparedness. But I shall tell you about the alarm when we reach the Wireless Section.

Come over here and meet Harmon, the Armourer-Sergeant. His is a very, very important job; he is responsible for all the guns in the squadron—about eighty in all—the bombs, the ammunition, the fusing, and the etceteras. Gunnery in the air is very different from gunnery on the ground. The guns themselves are practically the same, with the exception of the Vickers, which is air-cooled instead of water-cooled; but the belts, the make-up of the belts and the drums for the Lewis are much different. We use eight different types of ammunition, all mixed up in the belts according to the taste of the individual pilot or observer. The latter has one type unto himself—Pomeroy. Nasty stuff. It explodes on impact. Why pilots never use it is because of what might happen to them, or rather to the prop. Remember, they are firing through the revolving blades of the propeller. You can guess what would happen if a Pomeroy hit that.

While we are here and there is still nothing doing, let me explain to you the sighting or aiming. It is a most difficult job; you not only have to compensate for your own speed, but for the enemy's also. Yes, there is a different type of sight each for the pilot and for the observer. The former has an Aldis, the latter a Norman; both compensating.

The Aldis is a clever and efficient job. This is it —this tube about twenty inches long, and two inches in diameter. There is no time to show you its " innards," but inside are three lenses at equal distances apart. On one of them is painted a ring with a dot in the centre. When you look through the tube, this ring appears to be hung out in space. At 200 yards range it gives a diameter of approximately forty feet; that is the average wing-span of the Hun machines. The pilot's job is to get the figure of the Hun pilot cutting the rim of this circle, and heading towards the black dot. Then he presses the trigger. Theoretically, the Hun pilot and your bullets should arrive at the black dot together. When the theory works out, as it mostly does, you have some interesting information for your " Combat in the Air Report."

No, you can't waggle the sight about. You don't pull it down to your eye—the sight is fixed firmly on brackets on the top of the fuselage and in front of the wind-screen ; you use cushions, or adjust your seat so that in your normal sitting position you are always looking through the sight when you are looking to the front. The very fact of your looking forward means that you are sighting.

By the way, the projected ring is also an aid to calculating distance. If the Hun just fills the ring, he is 200 yards away. If he only half fills it, the distance is 200 × 2 = 400 yards ; if there is only a quarter of the ring filled, the distance is 200 × 4 = 800 yards. Get it ? By the way, the accepted maximum range is 200 yards. If you use a longer range, you give the target too much time in which to move. And, believe me, even in those days,

SQUADRON OFFICERS AT BELAH, 1917
(1) Major Williams, D.S.O., (2) Captain Murray Jones, M.C., (3) "Cam,"
... (4) Amber, (6) Captain Adrian Cole, M.C.

machines *could* move. Say you are doing 120 miles per hour, and say the Hun is doing the same. That means the intervening space will be closing at 240 miles per hour. Do you think you could hit a target moving at 240 ? ... No, of course you couldn't.

The enemy has secured not a few of these Aldis sights. But he is not able to manufacture them. You see, Aldis, the chap who invented the sight, put in certain gases between the lenses, at varying temperatures. The idea was to prevent the fogging of the lenses. But the gases also " fogged " Fritz.

Using this sight, there is no need to close one eye. All you see is this huge black circle ; it excludes everything else. When you get used to the Aldis you don't seem to sight at all. Just manœuvre the circle until you have the target in the prescribed position. Then you use your thumb, or thumbs—so. The rate of fire ? Well, the Vickers pumps out bullets at the rate of 520 a minute, and the Lewis at up to 460. But, as I shall explain later, the rate of fire for the Vickers depends on how fast or how slow your engines are revving.

Curious about this firing through the propeller, eh ? Well, I'd rather Sergeant Harmon explained it —he could give you an expert explanation. But as he is busy, I'll try. Interrupter gears, called after the inventor, Constantinesco, prevent the bullets from hitting the propeller—I will not attempt to explain the technical intricacies. But when the gun is linked up to the gear, and the gear to the engine, the gun becomes, so to speak, part of the engine.

The gun only fires when, and for as long as, the engine permits it ; and this permission is only forthcoming when the bullet has a clear passage past the whirring blades of the propeller. And, since it is spinning at the rate of up to 2,200 revs per minute in normal flight, and up to 4,000 revs in a dive, you can see there is not much margin. Actually it does not matter how fast your prop is spinning ; the bullets get through just the same.

Only two things bring about a meeting of the prop and the bullet : abnormally low engine revs, that is, anything below 600, which do not give the blades time to pass the path of the bullet ; and the other, faulty ammunition. . . . Remember what I told you about Pomeroy ?

Anyway, the control of the interrupter gears is fitted on to the joy-stick. To put the gears in operation, and at the same time fire, you only have to push down the triggers on the joy-stick. We call it " turning the taps on."

Well, let us get a move on. I have to be back on the job in half an hour. And I'm going to be mighty dry after all this talking.

This is the Photographic Section. Sergeant Coulson would tell you—if he had the time—that his greatest worry out here is water. No, not quantity ; quality. You see, ours is chlorinated—an anti-cholera precaution. That does not help to produce perfect photograph emulsions. Nevertheless, we do fairly well. We have two types of cameras—vertical and aspect. Vertical are far from satisfactory, because they are so liable to jam when the negative boxes are being changed. When you expose a negative, you have to take it from that box on the top, carry it over to the top of the camera and drop it into this box here ; that handle does the operation. Unfortunately, the sheaths containing the negatives sometimes stray off the narrow path. Then there is a jam.

And that reminds me of an interesting incident. One of our pilots, Lieutenant Taplin, when a member of a large flying photographic formation—five planes—came up against this jamming business. He was flying a B.E.12.a, a single-seater. As usual the camera was fixed outside the fuselage, on his right. He and his companions were flying at 12,000 feet and 1,000 yards apart, when his camera jammed. Flying the machine with his knees—that is, he gripped the stick between his knees—he dismantled the camera to adjust it. A Hun Albatros chose this very inconvenient time to attack him. Taplin turned and engaged it, but his gun being cold, jammed after the firing of one shot. " Taps," with his arms still full of camera, cleared the stoppage in his Vickers. Meantime, the Albatros had dived to come up under his tail. Taplin's gun responded to treatment and he turned on the Hun's tail, put a burst of thirty into him and down went the Albatros in a dive. Taps then completed the " roadside " repairs to his camera ; picked up his place in the formation, and carried on.

By the way, that particular photographic formation, in fourteen days, carried out thirty-nine patrols and exposed 1,616 plates, which supplied a complete map, accurate to the smallest detail, of 624 square miles of Turkish country. It was this little dump here which developed and printed the thousands of copies required by the Survey Section at G.H.Q.

Those prints you see hanging up there on the string line have been dried off with " metho." G.H.Q. want them pronto. Two hours ago that strip of enemy country depicted on those prints had never faced a British camera. Now here it is ready to hand over to the infantry and the gunners.

That's that. Now we'll see what is happening in the squadron's workshops. The main tent there is the assembly shop. Those lorries grouped around it are mobile workshops, each a self-contained unit. Among other things, they contain lathes, drills, grinders, generators, tool-chests. In fact, they can cope with any job the squadron may require. They keep all our engines running, supply us with electric light, and care for all our transport lorries, cars, tenders, and motor cycles. Incidentally, we have over a score of Leylands, fourteen tenders, four cars, and six motor cycles.

Now to the instrument-repairer's workshop—in this E.P. tent.

" Good morning, St. George. How's work ? "

" Plenty of it, sir ! But I s'pose that's what we expect in war, isn't it ? "

" If you've a few minutes to spare, I'd like you to tell this friend of mine something of what your job is in the squadron."

" Well, my section is responsible for the care and maintenance of the squadron's watches, air-speed indicators, rev-counters, altimeters, camera mechanisms, and bomb sights."

" By the way, you're a watchmaker in private life, aren't you, St. George ? "

" Yes, sir, and this work will keep my hand in, so that if ever this war finishes, I'll be able to start work immediately."

" Thanks, St. George."

You're intrigued about the watches, eh ? Obviously you don't appreciate the vital importance of accurate time—a minute can make or mar an operation. First of all, let me explain that all operations in war are timed to the minute, and the Flying Corps especially has to keep " appointments." More, we become official time-checkers to the whole front. Our W/T people pick up the noon time signal broadcast from Eiffel Tower at Paris. Then we make the necessary adjustment—depending on our geographic position—and check the result against the squadron chronometer. At various times during the day, the squadron will send out the time signal. Most of the units do not have W/T ; but they send in a dispatch rider with their watch to check against the squadron's chronometer.

This is the Equipment Stores. Have a look over the spares we carry.

This section contains everything from a Leyland lorry to a tin of bully-beef. And there are thousands of spare parts for our machines. Those two huge cases out there are chock-full of spare wings. Those smaller ones contain spare engines, and that there, as you can see, is a heap of spare props. Reminds you of a large ironmongery store, doesn't it ?

Now for the Wireless Telegraphy Section. You see it is some distance away from the flights. That is to get clear of the interference from the generators in the workshop lorries. We are proud of our wireless men. They are a great lot. This is Mr. Johnson, officer in charge. " Come on, Hec, do your stuff. Tell us something of your work."

Johnson : " I don't know where to start. But I take it you don't want me to bore you with wavelengths, spark-gaps, frequencies, and the like ? "

" Not to-day, thank you. Just give my friend here a general idea of your work."

" Well, to start with, we have eight detachments out in the front line with the Anti-aircraft Batteries —the 30th, 38th, 55th, 56th, 85th, 96th, 102nd, and 103rd. Our men's job is to co-operate with the battery commanders on their right and left ; to keep us, here at the home station, informed of all the Hun machines and their movements. When a Hun is seen, heard, or reported to be flying towards our lines, the operator at the battery transmits the message back here. Yes, by Morse. That operator over there with the head-phones on picks it up. He logs it, at the same time pressing that large black button opposite him, which sounds klaxon horns over at the flights—the signal for our stand-by machines to go into action.

" We have other jobs, such as intercepting enemy W/T messages, and forwarding the results on to the Intelligence people. Then we keep the mess posted as to news of the outside world. Strangely enough, our best source of information is the Trans-ocean service at Berlin. They transmit every night, and in English too. All we have to do to read their stuff correctly is to substitute the words ' victory ' for ' defeat ' and ' prisoners ' for ' casualties,' and there you are, you know as much as the next chap."

" Thanks, Sparks ! . . . We'll now stroll back to ' C ' Flight. See you in the mess later."

Come over and watch the chaps working on this Bristol which got mixed up in a scrap yesterday. There is no forty-four-hour week here. These lads work night and day to keep their charges serviceable. They have their own machines, one engine-fitter and one rigger to each, but when their own machines are all in order they always lend a hand to the other lads who may be changing engines or fitting new wings.

Parades ? Don't be silly ! There's no time for barrack stuff. The men fall in each morning under the sergeant-major, are marched to their flights, and dismissed to work. No more drill until they fall in to be marched back to their lines, at " stand down " at the end of the day. You see, service in a flying squadron is entirely different from that of any other unit. Here it's a kind of family team work. Each machine has its pilot, observer, fitter and rigger, and they must work in together to get the best out of the bus. Parade-ground discipline is non-existent. No salutes are permitted on the tarmac. And, thanks to the " Old Man," we have the finest collection of mechanics in the service ; he seems to have the faculty of selecting the right man for the right job.

Let's trot along. Here come the reco. machines now. Just watch and see what happens when the pilots alight.

" How's the engine, sir ? " asks the engine-man.

" Splendid, Jones, thanks ! "

" Rigging all right, sir ? " from the riggers.

" Yes. But you might take a little more slack out of the aileron controls ; I think she can stand it. Still, she's much better than she was."

" Guns and gears all right, sir ? No stoppages ? " from the Armourer-Sergeant.

" Quite O.K., sergeant ; had a No. 1 (stoppage), but that was when I was warming them. I soon cleared it with I.A. (immediate action)."

" Your Lewis all right, sir ? " (to the observer).

" Yes, Flight. No complaints. I think I'll put another $\frac{1}{2}$ lb. on the return springs ; this pair seems to like a high rate of fire. Take these empty drums from me."

Then pilots and observers glance over the wings with the rigger to see if any bullets or pieces of Archie have struck them.

" Fill her up, sergeant "—from one of the pilots —" and put her in front of the hangar facing out, in case we have another job. . . . Mr. Beaton, slip along to the R.O. (Recording Officer) and put your report in and then join me in my tent. I want to get your views on that ' private ' bombing target I pointed out to you at Es Salt."

" Boom-m-m-m-m-m-m-m——" roar the klaxons.

There goes the Hun alarm now ! Watch those chaps out there by 1229 and 4626—those two stand-by machines I pointed out to you on the tarmac.

" Contact ! " from the rigger.

" Contact ! " from the engine-man in the cockpit.

" Brrrrrrrrrmm." The Rolls barks into life. And did you notice she started first kick ? Those mechanics keep those engines " sucked in " in order to get a quick start. Here come the pilots and observers at the gallop. They have been enjoying a game of tennis on the squadron's court. They grab their flying-kit, but don't stop to don it—that's done while they are climbing to gain their height.

" Where are they ? " yell the pilots as they take running jumps into their cockpits.

" Flying S.W. at 16,000 feet in the Eastern Tactical Sector. The Archie batteries will put up ' pointers ' for you, sir, at 10,000 feet." (This from the W/T runner.)

" Right ? " The observers are in their cockpits.

" Right ! " they've snapped back to the pilots.

" Brrrrrrrrrrrmm." The Bristols take off in a climbing turn to the N.E. and continue to climb steeply towards the first Archie pointer.

And that's that—you have seen something of daily routine work on the ground. Maybe you will understand now why the various units in our little

family get on so well together.   After all, we are
partners ; all of us are equally responsible for success
or failure.   But, through no fault of their own, the
pilots monopolize the kudos.   And is it the pilots'
fault if all the nicest girls fall for them ?

CHAPTER II

AEROPLANES are like horses. Some are docile, reliable, well-mouthed, and comfortable to ride. Others, like polo ponies, are sharp and snappy on the turns, instantly obedient to a call for change of direction. Then there is the old knock-about type You have seen those old nags on general utility work —well-laden when the day's work begins, and thereafter needing the whip to keep them up in the collar. But when their nose is turned for home, they display a new interest in life.

Lastly, for the purposes of my simile, there is the outlaw, the animal which fights man's mastery up to the last ; in its record there is sure to be at least one victory, involving maiming or death for the vanquished.

Now for the aircraft equivalents ; the docile, reliable, well-mouthed animal was the all-purpose two-seater Bristol Fighter. You could use it for any old job going—fighting, bombing, reconnaissance, artillery co-operation.

At this stage I must tell those who do not know it that I am dealing only with aircraft on the Eastern Front. So far as numbers and variety of machines were concerned, they were very poor examples of the war's aircraft resources. Apparently we got only what could be spared from the Western Front.

Over there, they needed both quantity and quality.

But to return to our horse-flesh. The thorough-bred was the fast, single-seater scout, such as the Snipe or the S.E.5.a, splendid machines both.

The polo pony, not so fast, but capable of turning inside the speedier, senior thoroughbred, was the Sopwith Camel.

Then the utility horse. Equipped with wings he would be the bomber. Loaded up to capacity, bombers were always slow and sluggish on the out-ward journey. But you should have watched the air-speed indicator after the " eggs " had been laid, It almost seemed as if, with the day's work done, the machine had taken on a new lease of life, and was stepping it out for home.

Finally, there was the outlaw—the machine that had to be thrashed or coaxed into work. And, even in work, it had to be closely watched—for you never know what an outlaw is likely to do. Even if you did manage to get it off the ground, you could not relax your vigilance. Only when it was back in the " stable " were you safe. These were the machines that broke the heart of many a pilot, and drove in-structors to alcoholic consolation.

" What's she like ? " one pilot would ask of another who had flown a notorious machine. " Per-fectly foul," would snap the man who knew. " She's slow and sluggish, and she climbs like a brick. Give me old—— " (he mentions his favourite by number). " Now, there's a machine for you."

Machines are also like horses in this respect—

although they may be brothers and sisters, they differ greatly. Just as it is sometimes hard to believe that certain horses are by the same sire, so characteristics of certain machines differ greatly, though they are of the same type and built in the same factory.

I've read the foregoing over to some of my non-flying cobbers. They were interested, but puzzled about one phase of the story—

"What's the meaning of S.E.5.a and all that kind of thing?"

Well, before getting on with the story proper, let me explain a few things about the service aircraft concerned. The Bristol Fighter, or "Bif," was a pretty two-seater biplane, fitted with a Rolls-Royce engine of 190 h.p., and entirely devoid of tricks. She would not take a mean advantage of you by putting herself into a spin when least expected. She had a good turn of speed, good manœuvrability, and could carry a good load. In horsy language, she had a mouth of velvet, perfect manners, and no vices. She practically had no blind spots.

"What's a blind spot?" In war-time, a blind spot, my lad, is something in the build of the machine that enables the enemy pilot to bring fire on you from a point where you cannot return it because parts of your machine are in the way.

And now for the S.E.5.a. These initials stand for "Scout Experimental, No. 5.a." This machine was a product of the Royal Air Force factory, and was a single-seater biplane, with a stationary Hispano Suiza engine. Also a good-looker, with a sleek barrel. Providing you protected her tail, she was more than a match for the best Hun machines on the Eastern Front. An ideal machine, too, for ground strafing, for in this manœuvre you did not have to worry about your tail.

The Snipe, with its Bentley rotary engine, was thicker in the shoulders than its sister scout, and the fuselage, or barrel, was not as prettily slender. It was quicker in its turns to starboard than the S.E.5.a, because of engine torque, but in general performance it was the same.

The Camel, like the Snipe, was built by the famous Sopwith factory. She was so nippy that she could turn inside the Hun machines, and since she had twin Vickers guns, firing forward, and sometimes a Lewis firing over the top wing—that was left to the taste of the pilot—the Camel was a most unpleasant opponent. Probably, she was the most responsive British machine turned out during the war. A true story, told by a pal of mine, illustrates this responsiveness. He was flying a Camel over the line when he suddenly sneezed. Instinctively, his right hand, which held the joy-stick, shot in towards his body, and the machine made a perfect loop ! Any Camel pilot will believe that story.

Incidentally, the Camel flew as easily on its back as on its tummy. I would answer your " Why ? " but for the fact that positive and negative dihedrals, stagger, centre sections, and other forms of aerodynamic headache are involved in the explanation. These make heavy reading—and, *sotto voce*, still heavier writing.

To return to our non-technical Camel. She was not kind to pupils ; her very responsiveness made her dangerous in the hands of a tyro. As a matter of fact, pupils about to do their first Camel solo were warned that, if the turn was anything but good, the machine would immediately go into a spin. Consequently, a turn must never be made under 3,000 feet, and, as not a few pupils had bad memories, there was a very high percentage of Camel training crashes.

The Martinsyde was a single-seater biplane with a 160-h.p. Beardmore engine, and was a joy to the eye. But aloft she was sluggish, "sloppy" on controls, and altogether a horrible machine in which to fight for your life. Her redeeming feature was that she could carry a load.

The R.E.8, or to give her her full official name, the Reconnaissance Experimental No. 8, was also designed in the Royal Air Force factory. She was a two-seater, notable for the fact that she was one of the first British machines in which the pilot had the forward position ; previously the observer sat, or stood, forward. At last that individual had a chance to protect the tail, both above and below.

The top wings of the "Harry Tate," as the R.E.8 was generally known, extended feet beyond the lower wings ; and these extensions were seemingly unsupported. An unpleasant state of affairs, when Archie was popping about, or when you were in a tight, hard turn. I still get goose-fleshy when I think of those Harry Tates. No, they were not popular.

And now for the D.H.6. I hope it is as easy for you to read as it is for me to write of this dear old lady. She was the squarest old thing about the place—literally and figuratively. Square of wing-tips, rudder, fins, tail, elevators, ailerons. No rounded corners, and certainly no symmetrical lines. Her fuselage, or body, was just like a box, with the lid off. Of cockpits, as we know them to-day, she had none. Instead, a cavity which, in shape and dimensions, was like a coffin with the top removed. Hence, the " Flying Coffin," Also, the fuselage was not unreminiscent of the conveyance used on English farms to remove animal refuse. Hence a second nickname—the " Dung Hunter." The D.H.6 had an outsize in joy-sticks in the second, or pupil's, seat. When these fledgelings were in the early stages of their training, and found the movement of the machine disconcerting, a need came upon them to grasp something for support, and it was usually the aforesaid joystick which came within their grasp. And so another sobriquet—the " Clutching Hand."

In these days, when all the great Powers are working full throttle for bigger and better air forces, it may interest you to remember that a number of our machines in No. 67 Squadron were donated by the citizens of Australia—before we became No. 1 Squadron, Australian Flying Corps.

Here are a few I can remember, and their official inscriptions :

Bristol Fighter C4623 (N.S.W. No. 7).

RAMLEH AERODROME

No. 1 Squadron, A.F.C. in foreground. No. III Squadron, R.A.F. top left. (Snakes and jackals used to visit us here.)

Bristol Fighter C4624 (N.S.W. No. 12, presented by Government of
N.S.W.).

    ,,   ,,   B1148 (N.S.W. No. 2, " The
White Edenglassie ").

    ,,   ,,   B1229 (N.S.W. No. 11, " The
Macintyre Kayuga Es-
tate ").

    ,,   ,,   C4626 (N.S.W. No. 15).

    ,,   ,,   C4627 (City of Adelaide, pre-
sented by Mrs. Harry
Bickford).

    ,,   ,,   C4623 (Australia No. 20, N.S.W.
No. 18).

Probably the most popular machines in the squadron were 1228, 1229, 4626 (Bristol Fighters), and
4312 B.E.2.e. Especially 1229, which, I believe
earned more decorations in the war than any other
British machine—seventeen, I think it was. It
could almost be said that she was like a seasoned
charger—she only needed to scent a scrap to want to
be in it, and, once there, she did her part like a good
soldier. Fighting was not her only warlike quality.
She was big-hearted too. Twice she landed to pick
up officers of ours who had been forced, or shot,
down behind the enemy lines. She must have been
a crackerjack, for she was often lent to Lawrence, to
help him with his super-hazardous enterprises.
She was in the Lawrence class, too, so far as Spartan
fortitude and toughness were concerned. Many
was the time she was wounded, but never would she

C

leave the squadron.   Yes, dear old 1229 could tell some stories if she were not so unfemininely tight-mouthed.   Anyway, there is no harm in trying to draw her out.   She is in the Australian War Museum.   Then there was that invaluable old machine, 4312.   The C.O. used her extensively for transportation purposes—thereby showing excellent judgment.   But her most important work was test-ing.   She was the machine on which new-comers to the squadron had to prove themselves.   Graduates from the flying training-school were not straight away popped up into the air, to win the war in their first half-hour.   No, sir ! First the new-comer had to prove, to the satisfaction of the squadron C.O., that he could fly the squadron machines.   4312 was the test machine.   An old B.E.2.c, she was the vehicle that started many a good pilot on the right path.   Hers not the spotlight of action ; hers the drabber, but no less important, work behind the line.

I forgot another " horsy " comparison—the jibber.   I do not have to tell you what a jibber is in horse-flesh.   Well, the nearest equivalent, to my knowledge, was 4623—a Bristol Fighter.

Her history card read :

4623 Bristol Fighter M.K. iii.   190 h.p. Rolls-Royce ; Australia No. 20 ; N.S.W. No. 18 ; *The McCaughey Battleplane*.   Presented by Sir Samuel McCaughey, of North Yanco-Yanco, and Mr. John McCaughey, of Yanobee, Torun-dah, Riverina.   No. 1.

But for all her generous and exalted origin, 4623

was a perverse devil. Rarely could a job be completed in her, and, what was worse, it seemed as if she flatly refused to face the enemy. As a matter of fact, her failings became so pronounced that the squadron took action. At least, those pilots and observers who had been maltreated by 4623 did, for they held a court martial on the culprit, and sentenced her to six months over the line.

As a matter of fact, a big-hearted pilot took compassion on the " prisoner." A girl pal of his, back in Australia, had sent him a little gold goddess of luck. He presented it to 4623 ; the mechanics fitted Lady Luck on top of her radiator. "That," said the critics of 4623, " should fix the cowardly what-not."

The next day, the second of her sentence, 4623 went out on a reconnaissance. She had a good crew. Alf Poole was the pilot and Fred Hancock the observer. 4623 escaped. I mean she did not serve through her sentence. She refused duty under the plea of a conked engine. She was force-landed behind the enemy lines. The crew were captured.

As soon as we had expressed our sorrow at the fate of the crew, our thoughts, and tongues, turned to 4623. Unanimously we decided that it was a good thing she had gone, never to return. Also, that it was a mystery why the she-devil had not killed someone before she was " washed out." Yet 4624, 4626 and 4627, all sister planes, were excellent machines. They all earned decorations.

Another machine that was a stench in the nostrils was No. 155—an " Aspro " (Avro). As her number indicates, she was in the Methuselah class,

155 in 1918. Remember, her aeronautical colleagues were in the 4000s. And the treatment trainees had subjected her to had not improved her. One day, when the machine and the trainees had dragged the instructor down to unplumbed depths of despair and disgust, an old hand asked, in an innocently sweet voice, how 155 was flying :

" Like a —— Leyland lorry," snapped the instructor. And then, significantly : " Any of you fellows are on a couple of bottles of whisky, if she falls out of your hands . . . accidentally." There was an item of two bottles of whisky on the speaker's mess bill that very month.

The " Yellow Peril "—I've forgotten her number —was not the easiest machine to fly, but no one wished her any harm, with the possible exception of the enemy. Stewart Paul and his offsider, Bill Weir, could handle the Peril, and knew how to use their guns. I remember seeing, from a grand-stand seat, the Yellow Peril and its crew demonstrate how the job should be done. They were, or rather the Yellow Peril was, on the tail of a Hun two-seater. The poor wretch tried hard to dive away, but after Paul had fired about ten rounds it disintegrated. Just fell into bits.

However, the speciality of the Yellow Peril was a cavalry camp, and when it swooped down hectic things used to happen. I mentioned that Paul and Weir could use their guns. Because of it, this anti-cavalry turn of theirs earned them a unique distinction. They were specially mentioned in Turkish orders, as follows :

THE D.H.6
"The Flying Coffin," "Dung Hunter," or "Clutching Hand."

NIEUPORT SCOUT
Could they dive?

THE S.E.5.a
"It climbed like a tree-kangaroo and dived like a gannet."

THE R.E.8
The first machine to give the pilot the forward

All ranks are instructed to take immediate cover upon the approach of the YELLOW ENGLISH AEROPLANE.

Paul and Weir certainly wrote that name on the Turkish memory in letters of fire—machine-gun fire.

This individualizing of machines was not confined to squadrons in the line. They had similar experiences and tastes in the training squadrons. But the " Huns " (pupils also were known by this name because they were, in their ham-fisted way, just as dangerous as the enemy proper) were far more inquisitive regarding buses than the fully-trained pilots. This is quite understandable. These lads were, or should have been, feeling a very, very cautious way. Besides, the more a pupil can learn of a machine before he has to fly it, the less he has to learn when flying it.

God's gift to the trainee was the D.H.6, the dearest, kindest, most sedate old lady in a first solo. You could stagger " off the deck " with her, do the flattest of turns, and then just fall back on to the ground, and she'd still allow you to remain in one piece. She never seemed to mind maltreatment and indignities ; and she was probably the most uncrushable bus of them all. If she could have spoken, she surely would have said, " Alas, my poor aristocratic sisters ! Where do their looks and class get them ? "

But for all her forbearance, her sweet charity, and her many other virtues, Miss D.H.6 was always, as I said before, either a " Clutching Hand," a " Flying Coffin," or a " Dung Hunter."

And the ingratitude of the new graduates! After passing on to more advanced types, the fledgelings would never go up in the company of one of these dear ladies, not even to joy-ride:

"What, take you up in an old D.H.6? No, sir! Let me fly you in a real flying machine—any fool can fly a Dung Hunter!" It wasn't altogether ingratitude. You see, stunting was impossible in a D.H.6, and, after all, the graduate pilot did so like to throw his machine about.

Other types we had at our squadron were B.E.12.a's and Martinsydes ("Tinsydes"). Old 3345, a Tinsyde, was Fred Haig's favourite bomber. Fred loved that old girl. He used to fuss over her as if she were his wealthy spinster aunt. She responded to the treatment, and, on bombing achievements, Fred was regarded as the Tinsyde expert of our show. Old 3345 was slow-footed, but she had tremendous stamina, and she was absolutely dependable. I am sure Fred will agree with me that had he been flying 3345 on 1 May, 1918, he would have got away with his gallant attempt to rescue two of his brother officers who were down in the enemy's lines.

It happened this way: Rutherford and Haig, with an observer apiece, went out in Bristol Fighters, to reconnoitre the Amman area. Rutherford's machine was shot down, and, as per Standing Orders, the crew burned the machine. Haig saw the landing, came down, landed besides his distressed comrades, and endeavoured to take off with them aboard. But, just before he attained flying speed, a wheel collapsed and the machine nosed over. There was nothing else for it—she also had to be burned. Circassians captured the quartet and handed them over to the Turks, who later passed them on to the German Flying Corps.

Personally, I've had only one favourite. It was an S.E.5.a, No. A2.26, of the Royal Australian Air Force. This was after the war, and the only reason why I am intruding myself into the story is to record yet another instance of base ingratitude. I groomed and cared for that hussy in *de luxe* style. I spent hours and hours of my own time with her ; and quite a lot of what would have been cigarette-money was lavished on her appearance—varnish, metal polish, and little knick-knacks to improve her " turn out." Of course, I was very proud of her. But what did she do for all this loving care and attention ? She bit the hand that fed her. Actually, it was more serious than that, for she broke my neck. Still, I recovered, and she did not. So there is some justice. Exit A2.26. But, although I never flew again, and never shall, worse luck, I have this consoling thought about A2.26—I was the first and the last to fly her.

It is not exactly in the best of taste to round off a chapter on pilots and machines with stories of crashes, but this is where the following tale must be told.

First look at picture 4 opposite page 84 ; it is an X-marks-the-spot picture. That is not the mortal remains of one machine. That is, or was, two of

them.   Now the story.   We big-hearted Britishers
were called on to train all sorts of foreigners.   A
batch of Greeks arrived at No. 24 Squadron, and
Britain, dear old soul, said :

"Yes, we shall train you, even though you are
neutral."   Well, we set about training them.   It
was slow, exasperating work—their language was
Greek to us—but it supplied the Training Brigade
with one of its quaintest questions : " How are the
' apple-snatchers ' staggering ? "

First, I had better explain the " apple-snatchers."
The phrase originated from the Greek national
trousers—huge, blowsy affairs, that could have
hidden the crop of a big apple-tree.   And " staggering "—well, staggering was the word.   Those
pupils were a nightmare to the instructors.   After
fifty-odd hours " dual " (our average trainee was
soloing after seven hours), the best of the Greeks were
sent off solo.   Thereafter it was something like the
" Nine Little Nigger Boys."   You know : one did
so-and-so, and then there were so-many.   And so
on, down to two.

Well, one lovely morning the pair of survivors
were flying independently.   Apple-snatcher No. 1
decided to come in to land.   He made a fair
approach, but a little high.   His co-survivor, who
was just behind him, also decided that it was getting near lunch-time.   Incidentally, those blighters
would never practise landings—they would only
come down for petrol or tucker.   Apple-snatcher
No. 2 came in with speed to burn.   He sailed gaily
across the aerodrome and overhauled No. 1.   We

horrified spectators could imagine what was happening—both the trainees had their eyes glued on their instruments. Suddenly No. 1 glanced round and saw No. 2. On went his engine. At the same time No. 2 saw No. 1, and he, too, put engine on. Simultaneously, the poor devils must have bethought themselves of the hangars, looming like Mount Everests, immediately ahead. Both turned simultaneously. Yes, towards each other! Both turns finished at the same deadly moment—in mid air. Fate ordained that the wrecks piled neatly up right at the front door of the Salvage Flight.

Greece didn't succeed in establishing a nucleus for her Air Force that year.

Now, to take this nasty taste out of the mouth. At Point Cook No. 1 F.T. School had a tennis court, which was traversed, at a height of about twenty-five feet, by five big high-tension electric cables. They carried the "juice" to workshops. On the day in question, while a hard-fought match was in progress, the one and only pupil then in the air decided to land. He approached, straight towards the court. The game was held up to see how the budding Bishop would land. Hey! the stupid "Hun" will bend a wire if he doesn't put engine on—he's under-shooting to blazes. Just in time, the "Hun" realized his mistake, and tried to put engine on, but out came clouds of black smoke— he had choked the engine.

Swishhhhh! Nearer, and ever nearer, he approached the court. Hell! He's into the wires! Look out! The spectators on the court flung themselves down. Day-long seconds, and still no sound of the crash. We look up—there's the poor old Avro with her " feet " caught in the cables, and her " head " a few feet clear of the ground, looking for all the world as if she's hung out to dry. And there, blissfully sitting upside down amidst 30,000 volts, spread in four directions, is the cool, unabashed pilot !

" Hey, you chaps," he hails, " sling up a Gold Flake. I may be here for the night."

He wasn't there that long. But it was a most ticklish job extricating him. If you've ever monkeyed with a live wire, you will understand. The machine took a day to get down. And I'd like to have what that " arrival " cost in new fuses and blow-outs !

CHAPTER III

" HADJI "

I DO not like pigs. Pork, yes, and bacon. They
have their points, but pigs annoy me. There is,
however, an exception. It was a dirty, nondescript
little beast. I don't know where it came from, but
because of what its squealing terror did for me, I
hope it had an un-piggy end. I loved that pig.

I will never forget Rhododendron Spur on 15 October, 1915. In case you do not know your Gallipoli,
Rhododendron Spur is a ridge near Suvla Beach, and
its adjoining gullies, like most of those on that part
of the Peninsula, are deep, rocky, and fissured. In
one of them was a small casualty station. Personnel : a doctor, a sergeant, a couple of orderlies.
Accommodation : one bell tent, and the fissures.
In those blood-drenched, fight-for-your-life days, it
was a busy place ; and when I was brought down on
a stretcher from No. 3 Post, the staff was well past
perspiration point. Some cobbers of mine from the
divisional signallers carried me down. We were
good friends, but they were pleased to get away—
yes, pleased to get away from this comparatively
sheltered spot, back to a possie that German gunners
had ranged to a yard. For the doctor had said
" enteric," and although enteric does not sound as
bad as bubonic or smallpox or things like that, it is
contagious. If the burial parties had had either the

time or the inclination, lots of crosses on the Peninsula would have carried the inscription, " Died of enteric."

Well, the lads put my stretcher down, called out —from a distance—" Cheerio, Woodie," and went off.   I had been put in the isolation ward—a small donga off the main valley.   Another stretcher was there.   So far as I was concerned, the occupant was only a heap under blankets.   He had nothing to say.   Nor was I interested in him.

Merciful stupor followed.   Later in the day my stretcher was carried down to the beach.   The weather was bright, but bitterly cold.   A bleak, snarling wind thrust icy fingers throught the single blanket.   Hours, days, centuries, on the beach— by the watch only a few hours—and then on to a trawler.   It had been pressed into service as a hospital-ship because the casualty business had been exceptionally brisk.   A rotten little tub she was.   Later I was told she had been mine-sweeping and submarine-netting.   No pukka hospital accommodation, only a canvas shelter on the deck.   No beds.   We were probably lucky to keep our stretchers.

My fellow " isolatee " and I were carried on board and I can still hear the medical sergeant at the gangway saying : " Cripes ! here's a couple of infectious cases.   Where will I put them, sir ? "   And a querulous voice answering : " Put them anywhere, sergeant, so long as they are away from the others."

The sergeant, a real Peninsula graduate, soon improvised an isolation ward,   It was the trawler's life-boat—on top of the wheel-house, aft.   It con-

THE BRISTOL FIGHTER

tained a lot of coal-dust, some tins, bags, and a pungent smell. Our stretchers were dumped on the seats.

It was still " Unsociability Week " for the two of us. My colleague of Rhododendron Spur had not spoken. Nor had I. The width of the life-boat seats could have been the whole length of the Transcontinental Railway, for all we cared. The open sea brought us together—physically. As the little tub started to cavort, the stretchers would slide together and then apart. But no word from either of us. Not even when, as a wave tossed us about more than usual, there was a sudden and disconcerting movement in the bottom of our " ward." Something alive, something frightened and clumsy, was scurrying about. Finally, when it cannoned against my opposite number, and squealed in frenzy, the long silence was broken.

The other chap found his tongue. His voice, and the string of epithets, told me he was an Australian.

As further vicious bumps and wilder squeals called for action on our part, we both sat up, and simultaneously identified the nuisance. It was a pig. It broke the ice, and we started to yarn. Subsequently we learned that the pig was not a stowaway. Hard come by, he had been put there by the crew, with the intention of keeping him " isolated " until just before Xmas dinner. You could not blame them.

Now, I loved that pig, as I have said, because the chap he thus introduced me to was the finest pilot, the dearest and the whitest man who ever donned a flying-helmet. When he was off the

strength——or should it be " weakness " ?——of the
isolation ward trawler, he was a lieutenant of the
Machine-gun Section of the 3rd Australian Light
Horse.   Before he was last carried away on a
stretcher, never to rise again, he was a Knight of the
British Empire ; a captain ; there was a bar to his
Military Cross, two bars to his Distinguished Flying
Cross ; he had an Air Force Cross ; his name was
indelibly written in the history of war and of civil
flying ; and by him Australia had been placed on the
world's air map.   His name was Ross Smith.   We
officers of the No. 1 Squadron, Australian Flying
Corps, knew him best as " Hadji."

I have never earned a halo.   I have no illusions
about myself.   But now, nineteen years later, it is
my proudest memory that for eighteen months I was
tent-mate with Hadji, and that I war-flew with him.

Hadji, a native of South Australia, was college-
educated in Adelaide, and was in a hard-ware store
when he enlisted in 1914.   To us, who knew him
first in khaki, he was a solid lump of a chap, 5 feet 10
inches high, fair, and fresh-complexioned.   For an
Aussie, he had a fine command of English, and an
unusually impressive diction.   He had a loveable
smile, was intensely athletic, and was man all
through.   He was not a seeker of the other sex, but
women found him fascinating.   He did not avoid
them.   He was intensely fond of " Mater "——
as he called her——and to his close friends he would
often read from her letters.   A leader born, he was
absolutely fearless.   He was thrice valuable on the
Eastern Front, because, on top of his other war

qualities, he was a great pilot, a deadly gunner, and
he had brains.

Any one reading the previous paragraph will think
me heavy-handed with superlatives and their next-
of-kin. But I stand pat. Hadji, God bless him,
deserved them all. The official history of the
A.F.C. provides corroboration, and troops of all units
out on our front worshipped his name. Many is the
time I have heard Light Horsemen say : " Jacko
bombed hell out of us on such-and-such a day, but
Ross Smith'll fix the ———" (description according
to heaviness of bombardment). This unshakable
faith in him was general throughout the Anzac and
the Australian Mounted Division.

I am writing this book as a war-bird. Any one
(especially those who have never met one) will
tell you that war-birds were feckless people. You
know what I mean—flying off at tangents and all
that kind of thing. So, with this explanation—
certainly not an apology—I will start off with a late
story about Hadji : late in the sense that the time
was late in the war. You will find earlier stories
farther on.

Well, following the stirring times of the Big
Push the previous week, Haifa soon palled on No. 1
Squadron. That was in 1918. The swimming was
a great treat, but it made one get up on one's toes
more than ever. The fitter one is, the more one
craves action. Huns were at a premium ; we felt it;
our part of the war was on its last legs—we knew it.
Although we were not sorry, still it was irksome to
be pottering about without either enough action or

enough mischief. We did not know it at the time, but probably we were suffering reaction from the Nine Miles of Dead. I could still see those battered, terrified Turks striving, straining to get away ; striving and straining in vain. It had been too easy, too gruesome. I'll tell you of that campaign-winning butchery later.

Well, what we on the Haifa aerodrome wanted, and wanted badly, was a safety-valve.

Hadji had a brain-wave. He said to me :

" I say, Woodie, what about that dump at Jenin ? "

He mentioned it to me because I was one of the lucky ones who were in the know. During the advance Fritz had been chased out of his aerodrome at Jenin—all three squadrons of him. I had been doing a reco. The job was done and I was curious ; besides, I wanted some souvenirs. So down we came and then went exploring. Particularly, we had an eye cocked for Boche Z7 magnetos—there was an accommodating gentleman back in Cairo who gave us £20 apiece for them.

We had a special interest in this abandoned aerodrome, because we had " laid " numerous " eggs " on the hangars ; had fired thousands of rounds into the tents and workshops. Even without the excellent " maggie " pickings, it was a most interesting ramble. There were quite a few aircraft there, some whole, some the worse for our gentle attention of a few days before. We wandered through the hangars, picking up a thing or two . . . If you must know, a sand-bag full of Z7's. Then we had a look at the railway siding, where we found piles of war gear. What especially interested us were drums and drums of petrol in 40-gallon lots. Hmmm ! Wing H.Q. will be pleased to know that, anyway. The German hospital on the other side of the line yielded only a few surgical instruments, paper stretchers, paper bandages, and some gory " Exhibit A's." Fritz had probably left in a hurry.

" That cave over there ; wonder what they used it for ? The path to it is very well worn. What about it ? " Walking towards it, across a dry wady, we speculated. " Ammo ? " Bombs ? Special hospital gear ?

It was not an inviting place. The cave was in the face of a black, desolate hill-side. The entrance was about 7 feet high and nearly 5 feet wide. Miscellaneous debris immediately inside, and a lot of " dead marines." The cave narrowed, sloped downwards, got darker. Matches now. More empty bottles. What was left of the cave did not look inviting. We were just turning for home when we spotted a pile of cases in a dark corner. Forward the investigation department ! And both of us howled so joyfully that the matches went out. " Fizz ! " Cases an' cases of it ! Weinberg '04. And was it good ! My lips twitch at the memory.

No, I was not a teetotaller. Nor over-bibulous. But that stack of wine cases was treasure. Good wine comes easy to the throat of a war pilot, for hard work aloft, desert sand, and engine fumes generate a prodigious thirst. This was good champagne. A kindly German Government had

D

sent it to the East. Probably the War Lords knew that their Brass Hats or Turkish Allies would need a little stimulus.

Even if the name, or the vintage, had not impressed us, the fizz itself did. It was great stuff—easy as milk, full of tame fire, and squeezed dry of every morning-after-the-night-before kick. No, I could not tell how many bottles we drank, but bear this in our favour—we flew back home, landed in one piece, and where we hoped to land. And we brought a workmanlike supply of samples back with us. Had there been a popularity-competition that night, we were an odds-on bet. For we not only delivered the goods but told where they could . . . er . . . be purchased.

Ours was a dryish mess. The " boss," dear old Major (" Dicky ") Williams, was a hundred-per-cent. " dry." But he was also a hundred-per-cent. soldier. He did not preach " Be thou as I," but so far as was within his power, as president of the mess, he kept drinking down to the minimum. That, anyway, was his endeavour.

So, what with inaction, physical well-being, and vividly unpleasant memories, there were lots of visits to Jenin. And we always had a legitimate excuse. We could not say to our soldierly " T.T." Commanding Officer :

" Excuse me, sir, but the spirit moves me, and I'd like to hop over to Jenin for some fizz. Er . . . d'you mind if I take a machine ? " But you could ask for permission to go over for petrol. Our supplies were not exactly extensive, and there was that excellent Fritz fuel for the taking. Dicky liked his squadron to have plenty of spirit—aero spirit, that is.

These strictly business trips always had a spot of alcoholic colour. As a matter of fact, we called the home-coming planes " Silver-top expresses," because the observer's cockpit always wore a kind of hedge-hog coat of silver tops. You could rarely see the observer's head for the bottles stacked about him.

Well, as I said, one day Hadji had a brain-wave. He told three of us. We laughed and approved. Yes, we were " on "—it was an honour to be in anything with Hadji. We each had a job to do. Money changed hands. A Light Horse patrol at Afule had been grateful a few weeks before— we had helped the O.C. to pick up some important prisoners. He had previously located a cache of money : kerosene tins full of Turkish sovereigns and piastres.

" Help yourself ! " invited the grateful Light Horseman. We did. We were still well in funds when Hadji's scheme was put in hand.

I should not dream of saying that our accomplices were bought over, but they included a Railway Transport officer, a quartermaster, and an engineer-sergeant. After mysterious movements at several points, there appeared early one morning, on the railway siding which served the aerodrome, a captured Turkish truck. It was a small one-metre gauge affair, squat and low-sided. With express speed a 160-h.p. Beardmore aero engine, complete with propeller, was mounted at the front. Everything had been prepared—special engine-bearers, fuel tank, and dashboard. And the time, and the position of the truck, promised the minimum of unwanted observation. The engine installed, the hard-working conspirators nodded satisfaction each to the other. One of them took station at the prop, Hadji fiddled at the dashboard, and the truck moved off—for Jenin.

We were tired of " collecting " Weinberg by the mere cockpitful. This was to be a major operation. But, although we had excelled ourselves in the matter of equipment, there were two not unimportant matters to be cleared up. For instance, would the truck go ? Hadji, whose ear was stethoscopic so far as engines were concerned, soon settled that point. We moved off slowly, dubiously.

" Tick-a-tack, tick-a-tack, tick-a-tack," boomed the Beardmore, baritone.

" I'll try her full out," roared Hadji. The engine went all over basso, the truck shuddered and lurched. " Forty's her limit—at 600 revs," roared the engineer-pilot—he had to roar to make himself heard—" and I'm going to keep her at that." How he worked out the speed I could not guess. But he did tell us that " Agnes "—that was what we called our wine wagon—would have jumped the rails at over forty miles per hour.

I mentioned there were two not unimportant points to be cleared up. One was settled. The other was a poser. What about railway points ? This was a single-track line, and there were no sidings, branches, and what-nots, everywhere.

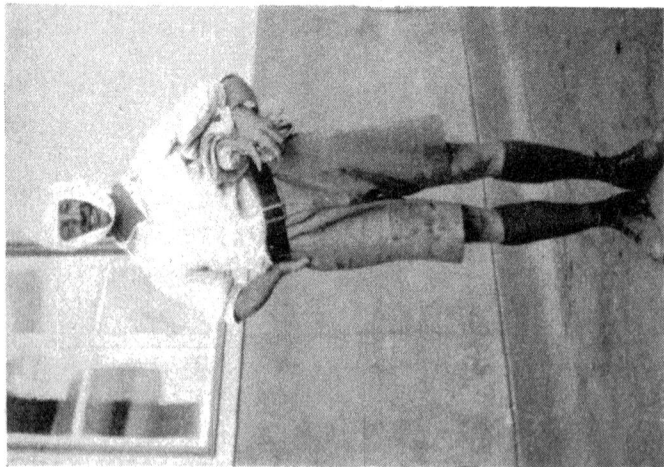

"HADJI"

And his Bristol Fighter, 1229.

"HADJI"

After "an air tussle that cost him some teeth and soiled his shorts with his blood. The bandage covers holes in his cheeks,"

What would we do if the points were against us ?
"Wait and see," grinned Hadji when the query was
put to him. His plan was working out splendidly.

But no. Agnes started to pitch ominously.
She needed a different weight distribution. And
when this dawned on us and we set about rectifying
the trouble, we made another disconcerting discovery. Agnes did not have brakes. Anyway, she
would stop when the engine was switched off.
When we had proved this, and had loaded a pile of
rocks into the rear of the truck, one of the crew was
detailed as brakesman. As soon as Agnes slowed
down, he was to jump out and chock stones under
each of the rear wheels.

But that was only a detail. We certainly caused
a sensation as we plugged along ! We were travers-
ing the Plain of Esdraelon, the Biblical site of
Armageddon—four modern crusaders of the air, in
what was probably the queerest vehicle that ever
desecrated those sacred martial shades. Those who
looked or laughed or cheered their astonishment
were much more interested in the vehicle than
its mission.

This latter, by the way, when queried by people
entitled to ask, was "reconnaissance." Usually,
our personal appearance was pass-word enough.
Three of us were officers, beribboned ones, and
Hadji's three pips, and charming but impressive
manner, were a good second line of defence when
necessary.

Hadji had to be very captainish and impressive
in Afule, a junction township twenty-five miles from

Haifa, for here the line was up. We ourselves had
bombed it to blazes a few weeks before. But the
sergeant in charge of the repair work was a good
chap ; he got a necessary stretch patched at the
double and set his Labour Corps people to man-
handle Agnes round a nasty corner. That corner,
incidentally, saved us from passing the railway
station. We did not want to go to the railway
station. There might have been important people
there ; they might have asked uncomfortable
questions.

And now for Jenin—nineteen miles away. Agnes
seemed to scent the hunt. She rollicked along in
splendid style. Only once did she stop. Ahead of
us, standing immobile across the line, was a Bengal
Lancer. His lance held out and up. That meant
" stop ! " We stopped. The Lancer rode up ;
four other Lancers showed up from an embankment.
The leading Lancer, a sergeant, saw our pips and
snapped out a salute, as only a crack Indian cavalry-
man could do it. Salute acknowledged by Hadji.

" We are on our way to Jenin," explained Hadji.

" Very good, sar." Another pukka salute and the
Lancers rode clear. They were there on outpost
duty. Bedouins were too apt to declare war, with
treacherous impartiality, on all and sundry. Out-
posts like these were an effective brake on them.

Jenin, at last. We pulled up opposite the remains
of the Turkish railway station, with such éclat
that the Railway Transport officer was obviously
impressed. He was a one-pip, blue-eyed young
Englishman, and when Hadji proposed a guard for

Agnes—Hadji called it a "railway mobile"—the guard was soon forthcoming. We had come, ventured the Railway Transport officer, to pick up gear left behind by the Huns on their two aerodromes? "Yes," replied Hadji, who was approximately honest. The Railway Transport officer was satisfied. Helpful too. He would be happy to supply a fatigue party. Offer accepted. But nothing conspicuous, no frontal attack. A dignified approach to the aerodrome. A short, but earnest inspection of the gear on the aerodrome. A casual saunter, minus the fatigue party ("stay here, men!"), to the cave. Stiffness! A guard!

"What unit?"

"Light Horse."

"Oh, that's all right," decided Hadji. "Just wait till I get my money-belt off—it's no use trying to pass dud Turkish money on Australian Light Horsemen; they know too much."

The guard sauntered down to the other end of his beat. And stayed there.

Yes, there was enough left for us.

"How many cases d'you think the 'hearse' will hold?" said Hadji. We, after mental arithmetic: "About twenty-eight or thirty."

"Right! Carry them out, one by one, and place them in the nearest tent in the German hospital. I'll take a couple of bottles down to the guard. Make it snappy!"

We got the consignment out; but nearly knocked ourselves out in the process. There was no sampling—a job of work had to be done.

The "Generalissimo, Weinberg '04," trickles back.

"Good! Now, all we have to do is to get the stuff down to the Railway Transport officer! Nunan, trot down to his nibs, give him my compliments, and tell him I should like a fatigue party of Gyppos to remove some . . . er . . . cases. About thirty men will do . . . What about a drink, chaps?"

We ceased only to superintend the departure of the fatigue party.

"Tell your *umbasha* to load the cases carefully in the *tiara* (aeroplane) railway truck."

Weinberg '04. That was a drink! Just when that grimy cave is coming all-over-Ali-Baba-ish, Hadji stands up. He looks his crew over, grins, sniffs, and then stands to attention.

"Officers, take posts!" he roars.

We take.

"Flights, move off independently! 'A' Flight, by the right, quick march!"

Nunan moves off.

"'B' Flight, by the right, quick march!"

Moore moves off.

"'C' Flight, by the right, quick march!"

Woodie moves off.

Marching easy, arrived in due course at the station. The Railway Transport officer smells a smell—there is a rodent somewhere. Hadji, however, is a great rat-repulser; Hadji, his three pips, his rows of decorations, and his smile. R.T.O. spreads himself, but he is anxious to get rid of us. Mutual back-slapping, and Hadji and his gallant

crew tear themselves away, and clamber unsteadily
into Agnes.

" Take post ! " roars Hadji, very captainish and
impressive.

" Petrol on—Switches off—Suck in—"

" Petrol on," etc., etc., from Hadji.

" *Contact* ! "

" *Contact* ! "

Agnes lifts her voice.

" How much gas have we ! " from Hadji.

" Not quite enough to get home," from Nunan
(engineer).

" Hop out, you two, and get one of those drums
from that dump there.'"

Up comes the drum—on Gyppo backs. It is
lifted into the truck. We don't need ballast now.

We move off. Agnes is beautiful. The weather is
beautiful. And the war and the trip. Everything is
beautiful. We toast our departure, our cargo, our
future, our hosts. This is a glorious, a marvellous war.

" Tick-a-tack."   " Tick-a-tack."   Dear old
Agnes !   Dear old—

" What the devil's this ? " suddenly snorts Hadji.
" The country has changed a hell of a lot since we
came down."

" Yes," agrees Nunan gravely, shaking a heavy
head at the landscape.   " And," with a change in his
Weinberg accent, " isn't that range of hills near
Messediah ? "

" By Heavens, it is ! " roars Hadji.   " What the
hoozit is up ?   Let's stop and work things out."

We stop.   The mystery is solved.   We are

going south, and away, instead of north and towards home. " Because, you —— fools," explains Nunan, " Agnes will only go in one direction. She can't reverse. I could have told you that yesterday."

" Well, why the hell didn't you tell us when we were in Jenin ? We could have used the Turkish engine turntable—if there was one."

Recriminations. Argument. Sorrow. As usual, Hadji came to the rescue. " We'll go south," he suggested cheerfully. Agreed. We celebrated. But as a reward for his discovery, Nunan was promoted to look-out—sitting astride the engine. Anyway, he got his share of Weinberg.

Everything was glorious. Along we rumbled for several miles. Then—crash ! When we sorted ourselves from the wreckage, and the roll had been called, we found that Agnes was fatally injured. She had encountered her first adverse points, and, valiant to the last, had jumped them. The engine had fallen out and the nose of the truck was buried in an embankment.

" Well, there's a road over there," Hadji pointed out. " Let's go and see if we can pinch a car." We go. We take a few bottles for company.

Up comes a Ford. Hadji signals. " Pull up, driver !—I want you to transport these officers and their kit to Haifa."

" But, sir, I'm to report at Jenin at once, sir," says the Tommy driver.

" Have a drink, driver. You must be thirsty driving along these dusty roads." Produces bottle.

" Thanks, sir. But orders say—"

" Never mind those orders, my man. This is urgent. And have a drink. And, Nunan, hop up and drive ' Liz ' over for your kit while the driver and I yarn about old times."

(Picture a Tommy driver, and the Ace of the East, a captain, M.C. and bar, D.F.C., etc., yarning about old times !)

Nunan returns with Lizzie and kit—as many cases as she will hold.

All aboard.

" Just a moment. How much petrol have you, driver ? " Driver was not sure—at this stage. " Right. One of you chaps fill up." We fill—from the drum souvenired at Jenin.

All aboard again, and off for Haifa. We detour round Jenin and Afule, and arrive at the outskirts of Haifa just on dusk. The Tommy driver is still with us. He does not care, now. On the contrary. When, after we quietly drive in alongside the mess and unload our kit, the driver is presented with a bundle of Turkish 100 " disaster " notes, and a Turkish sovereign, he is actively happy.

The squadron had just finished dinner. Our immediate pals were told of the doings. They had to help to round off the victory. Theirs the job of digging a hole big enough to hide the booty. But this was thirsty work, and the glad news spread, and we had to show our tangible appreciation of the congratulations. Further, it was hot weather, and we were scared that our cache would be discovered. So—well, what would you ? Agnes's cargo lasted one night.

CHAPTER IV

" BIFFY " AND " DICKY "

IN appearance, manner, and background, there could be no greater contrast than that furnished by those two big flying men of the East, " Biffy " and " Dicky." Or, to be more dignified, Colonel A. E. Borton, C.M.G., D.S.O., A.F.C., Commanding Officer of 40th Wing, R.F.C., and Major R. Williams, D.S.O., Officer Commanding No. 67 Squadron, A.F.C.

Biffy came to the Eastern Front, via Cambridge, the regular army, a Highland regiment, the R.F.C. and the Western Front. Dicky was a Moonta (South Australia) lad, educated at the local public school, who had gained a commission as a lieutenant on the A. and I. staff. Biffy took up flying before the war ; he went overseas with No. 5 Squadron, R.F.C., in August, 1914. Dicky took up flying after the war broke out ; he first went over-seas with the Australian Flying Corps.

Now it is impossible to keep up this contrast business indefinitely, so let us deal with each of them separately.

First, Biffy—he was the senior.

He had travelled far and fast, having gained his flight, squadron, and wing in under two years. Also, he had won a D.S.O. for conspicuous gallantry in France. He was boss of the 40th Wing when, in

JENIN : WHEN THE GERMANS HELD IT

Top right, two-seater aerodrome ; centre, portion of scout aerodrome ; right centre, hospital and
"'04 Weinberg cave."

1917, we manned No. 67 Squadron. He was good to the eye, was Biffy ; and good to the ear ; and to the soldier's heart. With his easy, straight-backed carriage, set off by a perfect tunic; with breeches cut as only an English cutter can cut, and field boots that would grace a field marshal, he looked the perfect gentleman-soldier. And he had poise, personality, and that something which hall-marks the gentleman. His voice was the kind one would have expected of him, although it sounded rather " what whatish " until we got used to it. But when he used to refer to us as " my Australians," and said it in a way which meant " and I'm damn proud of 'em," we were Biffy's to a man. A friendly, genial chap, too, without " side." He gave you the impression, when he asked you to have a spot, that he was taking you up to his rank—not that he was coming down to yours. And in things military, we soon learned, he was a big man.

Biffy's opinion of his Australians may be summed up by quoting the last paragraph of his report to the G.O.C. Royal Air Force, Middle East, which reads :

Throughout the period of my command, I have had the pleasure of conveying to No. 1 Squadron —one-time No. 67—special messages of congratulation too numerous to mention in detail, including messages from the G.O.C., C. in C., G.O.C. Middle East R.F.C., and G.O.C.s of formations with which the squadron had from time to time been co-operating, and I am extremely proud of having under my command No.

I Squadron, A.F.C., whose record is one of magnificent achievement—and worthy of the very highest praise.

A. E. Borton, Brig. Gen.,
Commanding Palestine Brigade,
R.A.F.

In the field.

I cannot remember how Biffy got his nickname, although the derivations of those of his two staff captains at Wing were obvious : Captain T. C. Macauley was " Toc C " (front initials) and Glogston was " Cloggy." Incidentally, not all the English senior officers had nicknames—usually only the ones we liked. For the spectacular side of war Biffy had no time, and with him ceremonial parades were taboo. " We are at war," he would say. " When we are through with that, then we can ' fall in ' and look nice." On one occasion, accompanied by Dicky and the Flight Commander, he was inspecting the squadron whilst the men were at work, when he became interested in one of the machines that had been badly shot up in a scrap. How many rounds had been fired in return, he asked. No one present knew, so the Armourer-Sergeant was sent for. The messenger, being a good Australian, decided to use his voice rather than his legs. So from the rear of the hangar he roared towards the tent of the Armourer-Sergeant :

" Sergeant, you're wanted in ' C ' Flight."

Sergeant roared back : " Who wants me ? "

Messenger : " Wing Commander."

Sergeant : " Oh, Biffy ? Righto. Tell him I'll be there in a jiffy."

Biffy, who heard all, turned to the Squadron Commander :

" Williams, who is Biffy ? "

Dicky flushed and looked uncomfortable.

" Well, sir," chimed in the Flight Commander, " that happens to be your nickname."

" Jolly good," laughed Biffy. And he went up another notch with the squadron.

But, although he was a great wing commander, Biffy was not exactly the finest pilot about the place. At least, he was not when the first survey of the England-India route was being carried out. Biffy was in charge. He had a big Handley-Page, with Ross Smith as pilot, and Shiers and Bennett as mechanics. A hand-picked crew, of course, and one that, with the addition of Hadji's brother, made the first England-Australia flight. Incidentally, Bennett was with Hadji when he made the Last Great Flight in 1922—they crashed when testing an amphibian for a round-the-world flight. Keith Smith, then, like Hadji, a K.B.E., saw the end.

But to return to Biffy. He was not a world's champion Handley-Page pilot, as the following extract from a letter I received from Hadji when he was at Government House, Calcutta, on 5 January, 1919, will indicate :

We had a fine trip over. The engines went perfectly and Shiers and Bennett looked after them very well. We had a slight mishap at

Bunder Abbas on the Persian Gulf. General
Borton landed and broke a bit of the under-
carriage, but we were able to repair it, and go on.
Again, on landing here, the General hit a tree with
one wing while taxying, but that is also being
repaired.

I cannot resist quoting again from Hadji's letter.
He wrote so simply, so frankly. Anyway, judge
for yourself :

> They all consider us tremendous heroes, and
> we have had a great time everywhere. I've been
> staying here all the time, so you see I'm moving
> only in the best of circles. I don't know yet
> if we are going on to Australia ; we are waiting to
> hear from the Air Ministry. I hope they will let
> us. I've been offered a job here with a motor
> firm; it's worth about £2,000 a year and it is very
> tempting, but it's not much of a country to live in,
> and I don't think I'll take it. . . . Doesn't it
> seem funny without a war ? This peace is an
> awful business, especially in Calcutta. It's jolly
> funny over here. Most people hardly realize
> there has been a war at all ; it hasn't hurt this
> crowd very much. Most of them have never seen
> an aeroplane, and at times I nearly bust having
> to answer damfool questions about the old Handley
> . . . I've been playing some tennis and golf, and
> took the General down at the latter a few days
> ago.

Maybe it does not sound very exciting. But if

you know a pilot as good and as big as Hadji, who has less of a " great-pilot consciousness " than he had, well, you are very lucky.

Sorry, Biffy, sir! Sorry, Dicky, sir! Hadji had his very own chapter and this is yours. I know you both loved dear old Hadji, but I promise he will not intrude again. Don't blame him.

Now to introduce you to Dicky.

After training in Egypt, he was posted to No. 67 Squadron as a flight commander in 1917. The squadron was still having teething troubles. The officers were a mixed lot. Most of the pilots were Australian, and the observers, wireless and technical officers, chiefly Britishers on loan. Dicky was an unusual chap. He did not smoke, swear, or drink. His most dashing expletive was " darn me ! " And he used to emphasize it by stretching and twisting his neck, or by another extraordinary facial mannerism—clenching the front teeth, and then a baring thereof. Both habits were disconcerting to strangers. Sartorially, he was the drabbest thing about the place. Every item of his uniform was " issue "—from cap to boots. No swank in Dicky.

But on one occasion the spirit of fun really did visit Dicky. That was in 1918 at Mejdel. He had his photograph taken, wearing a monocle. At the moment the shutter clicked, he produced that strange bared-teeth smile of his. The effect was certainly funny. You can see it for yourself. The snap is reproduced opposite page 56.

But Dicky (which stands for Richard) was a

E

grand soldier.　He soon licked things into shape ;
and there began that Borton-Williams partnership
which made aerial history on the Eastern Front.
Dicky forged the weapon.　Biffy wielded it.

But the fact that strangers found most hard to
understand was that Dicky was completely and
absolutely " pure."　I repeat, he did not smoke,
drink, or swear—and yet he was boss of a crack
Australian squadron !　Also, his sense of humour
was markedly under-developed.　He had no pals
or chums, and certainly no favourites ; he made no
attempt to seek more of one person's company than
of another's.　He had no bent to go wild on leave,
as we did.　He never joined in the pranks of his
squadron as did other C.O.s on occasions.

A splendid letter-writer, he wrote often, and at
length, to his wife.　Now, from all of this it might
be inferred that Dicky was not a man's man ; and
that he was unpopular.　Such an inference would
be quite wrong, my dear Watson.　Dicky was not
only popular, but he was also deeply respected
throughout his squadron.　For this neck-twisting
pillar of the proprieties was the soul of fairness.　If
Dicky held an " orderly room " and some individual
was punished, the squadron's verdict was always the
same : " Well, he must have been guilty or Dicky
would not have crimed him."　And that high opinion was enhanced by the fact that the subject of it
was courage to the backbone and a leader born.

He had an extraordinary memory.　He knew
every man in the squadron by name, rank, regimental number, old unit, and qualification.　He was

a splendid judge of men, and it was an education
to see him selecting officers and men from other units
to fill squadron vacancies ; especially when someone
was trying to play an "old soldier's trick." The
C.O.'s judicious questions would soon find a chink
in the armour.

Dicky was economical with bouquets. "Well
done," was his superlative. When you got that,
you knew you had indeed done a good job of work.
More comforting still was the thought that Dicky
was always behind you when you were doing your
work.

He had one habit that caused annoyance. He was
a "photographamaniac." (I made up that word,
but then it needs a new word to describe the lengths
to which this craze of his went.) Before he assumed command of the squadron, Dicky had done
a good deal of flying, and flying good enough to
earn him a D.S.O. ; and it was during this period
that the photographic bug had fastened on to him.
When he was put in command of us, it soon became
general knowledge that he was building up his very
own collection. But, really, that was only a side-
line.

As squadron commander, he had other matters
to attend to. Still he was insatiably curious about
the war, whether aloft or on the ground, and at
every opportunity he took or sought photographs.
Dicky was at his happiest—except when he had
learned that his squadron had done a good job of
work—when he could get up in old 4312 with a
good camera man. Thuswise he made not a few

trips along the front.   I can still hear some of the
observers snorting:

"Blast Dicky and his photos!   It's bad enough
to have to take them over the line, let alone 'shooting' your own territory just to supply some private
collection in Australia."

In March 1917 Dicky went out in a B.E. to
bomb Sheria.   Reaching his target he came down
low to drop his "eggs" on the railway station, and
was Archied heavily as he released his two 112
Hales bombs.   His engine conked, and after trying all the antitoxins he knew, he had a "close-up"
of Constantinople staring him in the face.   So he
slipped his flying-belt preparatory to making a
forced landing.   But as he looked over the side to
pick out a suitable spot, he happened to glance towards the engine switches on the outside of the cockpit:

"Darn me!"   They were off!   He switched on,
returned safely and made the necessary entry in his
diary—minus his customary ejaculation.

Dicky always tried to understand and help the
other troops, and the following is a typical Dicky
deed in this respect: During an advance in September 1918 our cavalry had moved far in advance of
their supplies, and they were existing on iron rations.
Dicky SOS'd the Comfort Fund People, and had
rushed to the squadron supplies of tea, sugar, soap,
and smokes.   We were mystified.   But before we
had a chance to investigate, Dicky called us together;
told us what the goods were for; and impressed on
us that they had to be got to the troops.   How to

"DICKY"

Major R. Williams, D.S.O.

drop them ? We experimented, and this is how we did the trick: tea, sugar, flour, etc., were packed in short lengths of a motor car inner tyre-tube. Not too tightly, or the tubes would burst when they hit the ground. The more important goods—the cigarettes, tobacco, and matches—were dropped per small silk parachutes. It was grand to see the troops down below eagerly watching the machines approach. Their very attitude seemed to say:

"Is it our turn for smokes ? " And didn't we tantalize them ! Cruel devils ! We'd show the 'chute over the cockpit and then veer off. But in the end we'd always do the decent thing. Ask any Light Horseman what he thought of those smokes from heaven.

To return to the Biffy-Dicky team. Early in the campaign Biffy must have learned that he had in Dicky a squadron commander who would go a long way. And he did all in his power to advance the squadron through Dicky, who, for his part, built up an organization that in itself deserved and demanded the most important tasks. Elsewhere in the book you may read of some of its accomplishments.

I must not forget to tell you about Dicky as a cricketer. He was intensely proud of his command, and assisted in its sporting activities; so we soon had quite " classy " cricket and tennis teams. The fame of the former reached G.H.Q., where Lord Dalmeny, Allenby's military secretary, was the cricket enthusiast. He organized a hot team and challenged our " Australian XI." The challenge was accepted and keen and regular practice ensued.

On the morning of the match, the team was submitted to Dicky for official approval. He was surprised !

" Darn me ! " he exclaimed. " Why, *I'm* not picked."

" But, sir," explained the secretary, " we didn't know you were a cricketer." However, the error was rectified. The team was not entirely happy about the last-minute selection, especially when he made a duck and dropped two important catches. But he was so keen that all was forgiven.

No account of Dicky would be complete without reference to his presidency of the mess, and to " Mimi." In furniture, ours was an excellent show —for a war mess. Souveniring had helped considerably, but the pride of the mess and of the ante-rooms were the home-made settees and arm-chairs, made by members of the mess out of sand-bags. But furniture was not the only attraction—our mess nights were also popular with all units, and were quite big shows. There were forty officers in the mess, and in addition there were our guests. Rationing was not the easiest thing in the world. Luckily our cooks always seemed to have, figuratively speaking, an extra ace or two up their sleeves.

But to provide a sufficiency of liquid refreshment —that was our problem. Remember, Dicky was a hundred per cent. dry; alcohol was expensive, and Dicky, as president, took a close interest in the mess accounts and bar stocks. Always the mess secretary had to submit the liquor requisition to Dicky. Without his signature the canteen would not supply

the order. So far as conventional details of a mess
night were concerned, Dicky was easy. He readily
gave permission for the show. He encouraged the
inter-mingling of officers, and liked the presence of
an officer of field rank. We usually had a general in
the guest list.

But that extra supply of liquor! In the form submitted to Dicky, the beer and whisky would carry
the figure 1, meaning one case. Dicky would
scrutinize every item, but after a question or two
would always supply the all-important signature.

Enter the villains. Before the requisition went to
the canteen the figure 1 had another figure prefixed
or suffixed !

Dicky was always an excellent host, and the best
mess etiquette was always evident up to the coffee
stage. At this point orders for the next day were
issued. Then Dicky would always excuse himself
and withdraw, followed by his flight commanders,
the latter returning subsequently to join in the evening revels. And what nights they were ! But
Dicky never remarked on, or complained of, the
noise in the wee small hours. He was very patient.
All he expected was that those officers warned for
early flying did their jobs. They did. But he was
always curious as to how the liquor stayed the distance.
He knew the capacity of some of his officers, and had
heard of the reputation of some of his guests. After
the Armistice, and just before his departure for
England, he was truly informed. His only reaction
was a neck-twisting and a " Darn me ! " A sportsman, Dicky.

And now for a word about " Mimi." She was a kind of marine relation to " Agnes," whom you met in the last chapter. Mimi was born at Mejdel. When No. 67 Squadron was stationed there in 1917, the enemy was depending on obtaining most of his grain stores from El Lisan and El Safiel, districts just east of the Dead Sea. The grain was shipped by motor boats some sixty miles across the water to El Bahr and the northern end of the Dead Sea.

To cut off these supplies, numerous bomb raids were made on El Bahr, with little or no effect. We had more success when our aircraft flew low over the Dead Sea and machine-gunned the boats, but the skippers learned to zigzag and they often escaped, with the result that Johnny Turk continued to get his grain.

Dicky was requested to give the matter thought. He conceived the idea of stripping a Martinsyde bomber of its wings and tail unit, substituting floats for wheels and giving its pilot-gunner an open commission on the Dead Sea. At first she proved a cantankerous beast. Her 160-h.p. Beardmore engine was far too powerful. She used to capsize at speed, and altogether she was most difficult to handle. Gunnery was another problem—it was impossible to fire over her nose. It was certainly a strange craft with a strange mission—the " Swiss Navy " could have shown nothing stranger. Mimi had to patrol an area of 800 square miles of water, 1200 feet below sea-level. Incidentally, the salt content of the Dead Sea is such that huge masses of salty foam were always in evidence on her " hull,"

Anyhow, all the troubles were eventually solved, and Mimi went out to clean up the grain boats. She must surely have been the weirdest craft ever seen on those age-old waters. The quarry was easily overhauled ; then the pilot would stand up on his seat and open fire with his Lewis gun over Mimi's tail—or stern. Probably her most effective weapons were her noise and her awe-inspiring appearance as, riding on a feet-high, swirling mass of salt foam, she bore down upon the enemy. Fanatical superstition did the rest—the " peaceful " Arabs and Bedouins never ceasing to call upon Allah when they saw Mimi at work.

Very soon the grain fleet was in such sore straits that reinforcements were sent to it from the far-away Bosphoros. Bigger, faster, and better-armed motor boats were transported to Jerusalem by rail and then carried by road to Jericho and the Dead Sea. And then, just when Mimi was proving too good even for these reinforcements, Allenby settled the whole Turkish grain problem. He captured Jerusalem.

If I were writing to either of the principal subjects of this chapter—and I shall probably have to when this book is published—the inscriptions would be : Air Vice-Marshal A. E. Borton, C.B., C.M.G., D.S.O., A.F.C., Governing Director, Napier Engineering Company, London, and Air Vice-Marshal R. Williams, C.B., C.B.E., D.S.O., etc., Chief of the Air Staff, R.A.A.F., Victoria Barracks, Melbourne.

The following incident has nothing to do with

Dicky and Biffy, but the mention of Agnes and Mimi makes it apropos. The story, like so many more in this book, does not figure in the official war history. It tells of another queer Australian-made war vehicle for which Nunan was responsible. Apparently Agnes and Mimi had inspired him. But he played a lone hand until the last stage ; we only heard the facts afterwards. Here they are :

Nunan was not only an engineer ; he was also a confirmed souvenir-hunter. Whenever he went out for a ramble he would bring something back with him. One afternoon he lugged back the breech block and the sighting-gear of a German pom-pom, which fired one-pound shells. He had taken these essentials in case, as he airily explained, some unscrupulous Aussie (we used that term, and not Digger as was customary on the Western Front) might steal the damn thing from the custody of the Salvage Corps. Later the remaining portions were removed from Aussie temptation. So Nunan had the whole gun and also a swag of ammunition in safe keeping. Then he turned his attention to the depot of the Inland Water Transport south of Haifa. This, by the way, was a naval unit. The " water " part of the name means not the stuff you drink but the water that carries boats. Lord only knows what the I.W.T was doing there. But they had lots of land transport, including table-top Fords. These were the attraction for Nunan. Once again he removed one cause of temptation from the reach of " unscrupulous Aussies."

By this time Nunan had worked out a scheme.

Why should such a fine cannon end its days in idle-
ness ? Especially when there was ammunition in
abundance. And why not have a crack at those
German rear-guard detachments and their machine-
guns—those gallant retreaters who were causing
spots of bother to the Australian Light Horse ?
Why not ? Things were quiet at the squadron.
But Nunan was a thoughtful soldier. Game, certainly—game as a soldier ant. But he knew those
German machine-gunners. And he was fully cog-
nizant of his lack of knowledge of the German one-
pounder. On the other hand, Nunan was very much
at home with a machine-gun. There was no chance
of borrowing one from the squadron. But Nunan
decided that he must have a machine-gun. Secondary armament, so to speak. So what ? Mr. Nunan,
incognito, again went forth to the dump from which
he had " rescued " the German one-pounder, and this
time he returned with a Spandau—a German
machine-gun. And ammunition. You see, we
officers had more or less " open go " with a fleet of
cars and motor cycles. It was just a matter of
getting a chit for fuel. We had eighteen machines
in the squadron, and rarely more than six were out at
one time. So there were always some officers free
of flying duties. Further, the flight commander
could grant up to forty-eight hours' leave without
reference to the C.O. And these were slack days.
Our part of the war was virtually over. In fact we
were so bored with inactivity that we voluntarily
instituted a Dispatch Rider Letter Service. We
used to act as chauffeurs for other units—carry their

dispatches, and their synchronized watches and all that kind of thing.

So after Nunan, his private armoury, and his transport had disappeared from the squadron there was no hue and cry. But when, a few days later, news trickled back that a Ford, with a German cannon and a Spandau mounted, and with a Flying Corps officer driving, was seen moving north along the Damascus road, we put two and two together. And, although intrigued, we did not worry about Nunan. But what the deuce was he up to ?

This is his own story. He had mounted the guns right enough. That was easy after powering Agnes. Just a matter of securing the mountings on to the floor of the truck. Fuel was another matter. Still Nunan had complete confidence in his ability to turn the trick. Confidence was justified. Soon after he made his getaway from the squadron, he came upon an abandoned German motor transport depot. The lorries and the cars were in a bad way —some bombs had found their target—but the fuel dump had escaped. A Syrian gendarme was on guard. But in the East piastres make excellent introductions and path-smoothers. When Nunan pulled out from the dump there was a 40-gallon drum of petrol on the truck.

So far, so good. Nunan was now within easy distance of the advance troops. It had been hectic work trying to catch up with the retreating Turks, and whatever units made contact with the enemy tore straight in. Johnny Turk had retreated so precipitately that only our mounted units could get

ENEMY MOTOR BOAT

Brought by Turks from Constantinople to the Dead Sea to wipe out "Mimi" (inset).

at him. And the German machine-gun detachments, which virtually constituted the rear-guard,
made it hard for our chaps to get at the main body of
the enemy.

No red-tape business in this phase of the war.
So Nunan had a scope which earlier would not have
been possible to a lone wolf with a queer wolf's
clothing.

One big problem remained to be solved—man-
power. Nunan could handle the machine-gun.
He thought he could use the one-pounder. But he
could not very well be driver and gunner at the same
time. Nor, even allowing for Australian military
elasticity, could he approach the O.C. of some unit
and say : " I say, sir, what about lending me a lorry-
driver so that I can run a private war ? " So
Nunan snooped about until he " enlisted " an adven-
turous soul who liked the sound of his plan. Nunan
never told his name. " But," said he, " he was a
damned good driver." The volunteer took the
wheel. By the way, Nunan had a name for his
vehicle—" Janet," I think.

Janet set out, looking for trouble. She took a
track that held no sign of life. Heavy going, but
driver and self-appointed artillerist were enjoying
contemplating the possibilities. Suddenly these became leaden facts. " Rat-tat. Rat-a-tat," barked
a machine-gun, and bullets whistled over Janet's
tail.

" Halt! " yelled Nunan. " Action front! "
Round swings the driver according to the drill book,
and simultaneously Gunner Nunan hops over to the

rear, rams a shell into the breech and pulls the
firing lever. Such minor details as range, angle of
sight, location of target and so forth, did not count.
" Bang ! " roars the gun, and a shell whirrs away in
the direction of Persia. Then the gunner sees his
target, one machine-gun, and he works overtime.

A pom-pom is about the easiest type of cannon
to use. The shell is in one piece, just like a rifle
cartridge and bullet, and there is no fiddling about
with fuses, or charges, or things like that. You whip
the one-pound shell into the breech, and the rest is
just a matter of aiming and pulling the doings.
Well, Nunan blazed away and——

" Did you hit it ? " we asked of Nunan, afterwards.

" No luck," he replied ruefully. " I hadn't got
the hang of this damned artillery business. But I
was getting the shells closer'n closer. Then, just as
I was a cert to hit the gun, the crew whipped it on to
a lorry and pushed off like blazes."

Anyway, the first engagement was a victory to the
Flying Corps. Or, to qualify it, a victory for the
heavy armament. How would the Spandau behave
in foreign hands ? Of course, Nunan wanted to
know that. And his driver, also feeling very bucked,
was willing. So Janet cruised hither and yon
looking for a nice private little war. But none
offered. Suddenly one of our mounted patrols
arrived on the scene. The chap in command having
a job of work to do, a one-pounder and a machine-
gun, both mobile, were a kind of military manna.
He ranked Nunan, and the need was urgent. So

Janet and her crew were enlisted. Thus employed, Nunan had ample opportunities to use his secondary armament. He stayed with the patrol until his ammunition gave out : then came back to the squadron. He had had his private war. He had won a round or two. Probably he had earned a points decision. Officially, Nunan had never left the squadron.

He returned to Australia with the squadron. A few years later, while testing a motor cycle and a side-car on Aspendale Speedway, Melbourne, he was killed. To his old squadron pals his end seemed like an anti-climax. Dear old Nunan !

CHAPTER V

Lots of people, liars included, have written about
T. E. Lawrence. We of No. 1 Squadron, Australian Flying Corps, were at various times his aerial
chauffeurs, his aerial lieutenants, his Arab impres-
sers. So I can, at least, write of Lawrence of Arabia
with some degree of first-hand knowledge. First,
some biographical details up to Lawrence's associa-
tion with the A.F.C. The following information
comes from various sources : Christian names—
Thomas Edward. Place of birth—North Wales.
Date of same—14 August, 1888. His father's
stock was Scottish, his mother's Irish. They were
not a moneyed family, but young Lawrence's brains
turned the educational trick. From the time he was
twelve years old, until he took his degree at Oxford,
bursaries and scholarships carried him through.
He was a bookworm, a keen archæological student
who spent his holidays in studying, first-hand, the
cathedrals of England and France. Almost, it
could be said, he lived during those studies on the
smell of an oil rag.

He progressed from cathedrals to castles ; from
castles to the crusades; and in the meantime he had
gained a scholarship at Jesus College, Oxford. He
was an unusual undergrad. He did not participate

in normal 'varsity life, but tackled only the individual sports ; and he made a positive hog of himself in the College Union Library. Often he would take out as many as six volumes a day—three under his own name, and three under the name of his father. That was the first published occasion on which Lawrence " put it over." Johnny Turk probably wishes that it had been the last.

In the long vacation, prior to his finals, he began the voyage that was eventually to take him into the front pages of modern history. He did a walking tour of Syria—exploring the castles. Academically, the first tangible result was the preparation of a thesis on the " Influence of the Crusaders on the Medieval Military Architecture of Europe." That won him first class honours in his Arts Finals, and also selection for the British Museum Expedition to the Euphrates. On the practical side, that four-month trip to Syria gave Lawrence his knowledge of Arab life, and an unquenchable thirst for more.

Again he went to the East, and his Museum work was interspersed with wanderings up and down the Middle and the Near East. In five years he knew Syria, its languages and habits, and he was very much at home in northern Mesopotamia, Asia Minor, Egypt, and Greece. Also he had become extraordinarily expert in the various dialects of the peoples inhabiting those lands.

" Particularly my poverty let me learn the masses, from whom the wealthy one was cut off by his money, and his attendants," wrote Lawrence of this sojourn in the Near East. The experience he

F

gained was the basis of what was afterwards his unique power.

In those days, as in the days when we knew him, Lawrence was short, fair, blue-eyed, slight, and clean shaven. The upper part of his face was kindly, but the lower part severe, perhaps cruel. In physique and colouring he was in marked contrast to the Arabs, who were big fellows, tall, dark, and bearded.

> Among the Arabs there were no distinctions [wrote Lawrence], traditional or natural, except the unconscious power given a famous sheikh, for something done. They taught me that no man could be their leader, except he ate their food, wore their clothes, lived level with them, and yet appeared better in himself.

Obviously Lawrence set out to achieve leadership. He lived, dressed, talked, and ate as an Arab. He must have done it thoroughly ; because on one occasion, whilst travelling along the valley of the Upper Euphrates, he and a workman companion were arrested as suspected deserters from the Turkish army. Bribery got him out of a dungeon.

By 1913 Lawrence had very definite views about international politics in the East. And he must have cut some ice out there. For in Cairo he called on, and was received by, no less a personage than Kitchener. Lawrence wanted to know why Germany had been allowed to get control of Alexandretta. Obviously, the little archæologist was not very keen about the Germans—his own story gives his views in detail, as well as Kitchener's reply to his query—for when he returned to Carchemish, Syrian base of the British Museum activities, he launched a pungent practical joke on the Germans. He caused sections of drain-pipes to be loaded on mule-back, and carried to the hills which looked down on the German-built railroad. There they were so mounted on piles of sand that the German engineers, investigating by field glasses, mistook them for guns—British guns. And from Constantinople Berlin received urgent and disquieting news that the British were fortifying the hills on both sides of the railway line.

A few months later, when back in London, Lawrence's anti-Germanism became intensified. War had been declared, and Lawrence wanted to be in it. He tried to enlist in " Kitchener's Mob," but the doctors said " No." Grow up and wait, they said, and then there might be another war. At twenty-five he was still a little, insignificant-looking chap. And in those days the army doctors only accepted man-sized men. The reject returned to his ruins, and stayed there, until he had a job wangled for him in the Map Division of the Intelligence Department at G.H.Q., Cairo. It carried one pip. But Second-Lieutenant Lawrence was a very handy man. He knew many of the roads and routes on that front, and he knew that not a few of the Army maps were sadly incorrect, in spite of the fact that the surveyors had included one Lieutenant Kitchener. That was the Commander-in-Chief's rank when the Royal Engineers made the maps.

There was another department at G.H.Q. that
dealt with the situation behind the enemy's lines.
It was after Lawrence had been transferred there-
to, and had got a stomachful of " red tape," that
something happened which was to affect vitally the
Eastern Front. Grand Sherif Hussein, his four
sons, and their Arab followers in the Hejaz, re-
volted against Turkey. They captured Mecca, were
defeated at Medina, and withdrew into the hills to
cover the Mecca road. From which point they applied to Britain for assistance. Britain couldn't hear,
or wouldn't. Second-Lieutenant Lawrence could
and did. He applied for fourteen day's leave, and
got it. So far as G.H.Q. was concerned, Lawrence
made that leave last until the end of the war. But
the leave began quite unimpressively. He went to
Jeddah, on the Red Sea, secured a camel and went
forth to find Emir Feisal, third son of the rebel-in-
chief, who was doing his utmost to keep the other
rebels rebellious.

When Lawrence, complete with one camel, man
and beast very much the worse for wear, located
him, things were not over-promising. Feisal did
not have enough ammunition to keep his army in
meat, and they were living on locusts and wild
honey—a most unsatisfactory diet for fighting men.
However, Lawrence had a plan, and the rebel
leader accepted it. Lawrence was convinced that
the Arabs could be organized into " regular irregulars," who could assist the British in Egypt and
Syria. But the first move was so to equip the
Bedouins in the hills between Medina and Rabegh

that they would be able to hold up the Turks while the Arabs were being organized. However, the Bedouins could not, and did not, stop Johnny Turk, and when Lawrence was down with fever in Rabegh Johnny came up on the run. Exit Feisal, Lawrence, and all except Feisal's youngest brother Zeid, who was left with a few Bedouins to harass the Turks.

Followed a game of hide-and-seek, with Lawrence hatching a deep and most ambitious scheme. The Turks had a force of 100,000. The rebel forces were outnumbered, out-armed, out-equipped. But this a.w.l. one-pip strategist decided that, if the non-rebelling Arabs could be convinced that it was up to them to fight for the breaking of the Turkish yoke and that this liberation could only be effected by forgetting tribal differences and internecine brawls, then the Turks were in for a rough time. Lawrence set out to raise the standard of rebellion. With 240 men he traversed the desert, visiting every camp, and in the name of Feisal talking his war talk. He spoke excellent Arabic, and the name of Feisal was his talisman. For a Christian, an infidel, on sacred Arabian soil, it was a most dangerous mission. But it succeeded. Within six months nearly all the tribes were up and doing, and united against the common enemy.

All that is history. Now I want to give you a personal " close-up " of Lawrence the man, in the hope that it may help you better to understand him, before the story gets too far into its stride.

Early in 1916 I was sitting in the *patio* of Shepheard's Hotel with an R.E. officer, when another officer passed along the *sharia* (street). He was so small and so extraordinary-looking that I asked the engineer who he was.

"That's Second-Lieutenant Lawrence of the Map Division of G.H.Q. A peculiar sort of chap, but, believe me, he knows his East."

The first time I met Lawrence in person was in May, 1918, at Ramleh aerodrome. He was returning a call on Allenby at his headquarters at Richon, and was awaiting a Bristol in which Ross Smith was to fly him to Kutrani. He was a different Lawrence from the queer little officer I had seen in Cairo. Now he was a cut-down Arab, a midget sherif. He wore Arab togs, complete even to bare feet; but he was a Hop-o'-my-Thumb compared with the genuine Arabs. Lawrence was about 5 feet 3 inches in height, and he looked far less than the 9 stone he weighed. He told me his measure and weight when I got to know him. He had blue eyes. And what eyes! If I were a talkie-star of the coloured screen, I'd give five years peak-salary for a pair of MKv.a Lawrence grade optics.

"Sherif Aurans"—which was the nearest the Arab tongue could get to Lawrence—also had a remarkable pair of hands. For slender, shapely beauty, they, too, were unique. Lawrence was proud of them. When you worked for, and with, him at close quarters, as some of us did, you soon got to know this by the meticulous attention he devoted to them. But, as we soon learned, those hands were for use, not for ornament. They were almost incredibly strong. I have winced at his grip, and, feeling much more comfortable, have seen them doing things to other people.

In wrestling, for instance, I've seen this little stripling of a chap—a bantam, who could not have joined the A.I.F. as a batman to a padre—throw and pin big Arabs almost twice his weight. And the opposition was not " pulling its punches."

The Arabs are one hundred per cent. keen about feats of strength, fitness, and all that kind of thing, and the thought of being worsted by a little white man, even though he was a great soldier, was not pleasing. Of course, Sherif Aurans did not win his wrestling bouts by the strength of his hands alone. He was piano wire, and whipcord, and eel—and he had a split-second brain.

Only we chaps who flew with Lawrence's " Air Force," saw, and fully appreciated, this physical side of him. We had plenty of chances, especially after " dinner " on the days when there was no fighting or planning to be done. There would be talk, and then Lawrence and a volunteer would strip to their pants and " rassle " on the sand. I have often wondered since then, after hearing and seeing some of these allegedly " all-in " professional wrestlers moan in anguish and howl and gesticulate, what would happen if a Lawrence met one of them on the mat—Lawrence, his normally homicidal self, and the " pro " doing showman stuff.

Lawrence was a dandy in his quiet way. So far as it could be said of Arab clothes, they fitted him perfectly, and except when he was masquerading behind the enemy lines, they were always spotlessly white. The only touches of colour that bespoke the Arab sherif were in his head-rope and girdle, and the ceremonial gold dagger at his waist.

His best " suit " had a history, with possibly a smile behind it. Feisal gave it to him. Ordinarily, it would have been a particular mark of distinction, for this was Feisal's wedding-gown. Or rather, as was the Arab custom, it had been given to Feisal by his mother, as a reminder that he was of marriageable age. Probably the Arab idea was that in such glorious raiment—it was bejewelled and gold-embroidered—the recipient would be irresistible. But charming, quaintly slim Feisal had been Westernized. He had been to Oxford, and all that kind of thing, and although no Arab could have been more Arabian in the fight he so grandly waged, at least in this matter of the " wedding reminder " he was the Occidental, rather than the Eastern, bachelor. Anyway, he gave his mother's present to Lawrence. The initial significance of the robes was wasted on him also ; but I have often wondered whether Feisal honoured his adviser-friend with malice aforethought.

And that reminds me. Any girl lucky enough to have blue eyes of Lawrence shade should always wear white. A grand combination.

I mentioned a dagger. Never, except on his " tulip " expeditions, mentioned hereafter, did Lawrence wear any other weapon. Not even when, as the dramatic writers put it, he ventured into the lion's den—when he was snooping solo, hundreds of miles behind the enemy's lines. Why didn't he carry a revolver? Lawrence never told us, but I think it was because he had entered so closely into Arab life that, while he was an Arab chief, an Arab chief he determined to be in every slight detail. And Arab chiefs in those days did not " tote guns."

For that reason Lawrence wore no footwear. That was also a quaint old Arab custom. Incidentally, Lawrence's feet were, like his hands, slim and unmasculinely beautiful.

Whatever else their failings, the Arabs were tremendously tough. On camel-back they could cover huge distances, day after day, night after night, existing the while on the smell of an oil rag. Have you ever ridden a camel? Until you've mastered the art, it is a painful stomach-straining experience, even for a veteran horseman. The Arabs are probably the best cameliers in the world. Yet Aurans could stay and pace it with the best of them. He was always splendidly mounted, as befitted his Arab rank, and Ghazala (his favourite she-camel) could pace and last it with any beast of what became the biggest irregular force of the war.

Ghazala was given to Aurans by Feisal. She was pure white, a thoroughbred dromedary, ranking as high as the proudest pedigreed Arab horses. I've seen some good rough riders, bush riders and the like, in my time, but I've never seen a more exhilarating riding-stunt than Lawrence doing one of the Arab tests with Ghazala. This was to dismount at the gallop, rifle in hand, and then mount again, still rifle in hand, without slackening pace. It doesn't sound so hard, but remember that Ghazala was about 6 feet high, her saddle was 5 feet 6 inches from the ground, and Lawrence was a little slip of a bantam. Remember, also, that he had only one hand with which to lower and raise himself to and from the saddle, and a rifle is not exactly thistle-down in an act like that.

I have referred to Lawrence's stamina. Here is an instance of what he, and Ghazala, could do. It was a rush job—Lawrence had to get in personal touch with British H.Q. at Suez. So, with twenty-one members of his personal bodyguard, he set out to cover the miles of desert, from Akaba. This bodyguard was made up of hand-picked members of the various tribes fighting the good fight. These were indeed fighting men, fanatically proud of their job, fanatically true to their trust. Well, Aurans set out in a hurry. It was intensely hot by day, bitterly cold at night, and Aurans would not, could not, stop even for food. Only one man got through. Yes, you will have guessed right. What of the others? They were desert men, and they could look after themselves—that is, if " neutral " Bedouins and belligerent Turks were not looking harder. Anyway, on jobs like that, the individual did not count where the mass was concerned.

There was a funny incident connected with his return trip from Suez. He was still in Arab garb, but he had an official permit. The Red Caps at the station were suspicious. They did not seem to mind his white silken robes, his gold rope and be-jewelled dagger, but one pair of eagle eyes espied bare feet. That, or they, were apparently a bad thing. The suspect was quite frank. The uniform he was wearing was that of a staff officer to the Sherif of Mecca. " Never heard of it, and don't know the uniform," remarked the sergeant. Those military policemen could be very direct, especially if the other chap was not important, and there was no one important within range.

" Well," said Lawrence—I'm sure his blue eyes were glinting—" would you know the uniform of a Montenegrin dragoon ? "

That was too much for the Red Caps. They withdrew. But the sergeant wired his suspicions up the line, where an Intelligence officer—an intelligent one—was very angry to find he had been called in on a fool's errand.

That mordant touch in Lawrence's retort was typical of the man when he was annoyed. He was at his best—or should I say his worst—in three verbal clashes with women, of which we chaps heard. We used to chuckle hugely over the stories, but the victims . . . well, I don't know whether that term is right. Anyway, I'll tell the stories and you can judge for yourself. During his later and more publicized activities in Arabia, Lawrence was very much a social lion. He loathed the rôle, but society in Cairo especially did its best to rope him in and make him roar. Roar, lion-style, that is.

The big occasion in those days was the Wednesday afternoon dance at Shepheard's. This was a joint effort by the womenfolk of Cairo—English, French, and Italian social headliners, mostly married, who issued the invitations, and who judging by their

actions, were vastly concerned about finding a hus-
band, preferably an Englishman, for daughter.
Bright young officers were usually the guests. But
one afternoon an indefatigable worker roped in
Lawrence, and at her arrangement the band struck
up " See the Conquering Hero Comes," as he
entered. The lion was unaware of the musical
honour being paid him, but when Madame President
set out on a speech appropriate to the occasion, Lawrence's face darkened with anger and finally he
interrupted :

" Madame," he said, " my first pleasure when I
return to the Arabs will be to acquaint them of the
fact that in Cairo there exists an organization of old
women who have not yet learned that there is a war
in existence."

Then he stalked out. Next to having Lawrence
as a guest, it was the ambition of many Cairo ladies
to speak to the lion in public and to be seen so doing.
One hot afternoon Lawrence and a friend were
standing talking in the *patio* of the Continental
Hotel when up bustled a lady of not-so-tender years
fanning herself vigorously and said :

" Ninety-two, to-day, Colonel Lawrence. Think
of it—ninety-two ! "

" Many happy returns of the day, madame,"
replied Lawrence, smiling. The villain in that
piece himself told us that story. And Sir Ronald
Storrs told this one. When Sir Ronald was gover-
nor of Jerusalem, a well-known social lady, newly
arrived from England, was a guest at a dinner and so
was Lawrence. The lady seen let all and sundry

know that she was very much a Somebody. She referred to duchesses by their Christian names, countesses by their pet names, and baronesses by their nicknames. She monopolized the conversation in a heavy *on dit* fashion. The other guests looked bored, but Lawrence's face and manner registered definite disapproval. This the floor-holder suddenly noticed. She pulled up :

" I am afraid," she said, " my anecdotes do not interest Colonel Lawrence particularly."

" Particularly ? " repeated Lawrence, " Why, the anecdotes do not interest me at all ! "

And there was the occasion on which Lawrence turned an edged tongue at a neighbouring squadron. One of their machines, on its way to bomb the Hejaz railway, was fired on from the ground while passing over the north end of the Dead Sea. The crew noted the spot, and to return the courtesy kept a bomb for the return trip. The bomb was dropped. That was that. But it was more. Later in the day there was consternation in the squadron. A message had come through telling that a British machine had bombed Lawrence's bodyguard, nearly wiping it out. Details of time and place convicted the machine that had returned the ground courtesy.

When a few days later Lawrence himself came to the squadron the worst fears seemed justified. But he was quite friendly when he discussed the matter in the mess. There had been a misunderstanding, he said. His bodyguard had fired at the machine merely out of light-heartedness. A kind of welcome —*feu de joie*. No malice. So that they were quits

about the bombing ; " because," added Lawrence
sweetly, " the aim was so rotten that the bombing did
not really matter ! "

So far as the British Government was concerned,
Lawrence became a personage from the day when
he was awaiting a train at Ismailia ; he was bound for
Cairo, after a forced march across the desert to Suez.
I have heard versions of the incident from several
eyewitnesses and participants, Lawrence included,
and this is how I fit the pieces together :

Another train pulled in, and an admiral and three
high-ranking staff officers stepped out and began a
" constitutional " on the railway platform.   One of
them saw Lawrence, or rather Aurans—he was in
Arab garb—whom he knew, and went over to him.
The officer was an A.D.C.

" Who is the Brass Hat aboard? " asked Lawrence.

" That," said the A.D.C. with due respect, " is
General Allenby, the newly appointed G.O.C."

" Oh," said Lawrence, non-committally, and
resumed his leaning position against a wall.   Lawrence heartily disliked Brass Hats.   They had
failed him, when their help would have been so
important to the cause of Feisal, and to Britain ; and
while he was at headquarters he had convincing
evidence of some types of high-ranking brain.   Or
rather, of the brains of high officials.   So far as the
numbers were concerned, Lawrence told us that on
one occasion he and a soured fellow-subaltern lurked
behind a screen at Shepheard's, and in one afternoon
counted no fewer than sixty-five generals.

While back at Cairo for a moment, I may as well

tell you how Lawrence came to get away from the swathes of red tape, and the " dogs on the cushions," and all that kind of thing, at headquarters. As I mentioned before, he was invaluable. He tried, at every opportunity, to get away and be a real soldier. He applied for transfers. No! came the reply. He applied for leave : the same reply. These applications for leave were only a blind. Lawrence wanted to get away from the whole thing. He wanted to soldier, not to clerk.

After the umpteenth " knock back " to his applications he conceived a more crafty method. This is how he worked. At that time Lawrence was recognized as the final authority on roads and routes, wadys, water-supplies, and so forth, in the war area. If ever there was a doubt about the correctness of the maps—and, as the authorities learned to their cost, many of the official maps were far from reliable —Lawrence was called on to elucidate. The map, or whatever it was, would be sent to him for report.

Instead of righting the wrongs, he would confine himself to criticizing the English of either the original document or of the " please-explain " of the officer calling for the report. Nor did he pull his punches. He would point out that a sentence should not end with a preposition, or that a split infinitive was " not done," and so on. And the corrections and admonitions were always in red ink. One can understand the feelings of the high officer thus rebuked by a stripling whose badly worn uniform carried only one pip. It was all so very unmilitary. Anyone else but a Lawrence would have been pulled up with the shortest of jerks. But H.Q. was having a very unhappy time, and Lawrence was the only man who was *au fait* with one of the most ticklish of its problems. But this literary criticism, coupled with the outrageous insolence behind it, so stung the high-ranking hide that when next Lawrence applied for leave it was granted. So Lawrence, his blue eyes a-twinkle, went forth, never to return as second-lieutenant. As a matter of fact, this leave began what was probably the most extraordinary story of its kind in the history of the war.

Lawrence went away on fourteen days' leave, and never returned. Ordinarily, that would have been interpreted as desertion, for which the maximum penalty was death. But there was no blank wall and firing party for this man, technically guilty of one of the most serious crimes in the army calendar. Promotion, not punishment, was the result. While he was still officially a.w.l., Lawrence was made a full colonel. He skipped four ranks in one swoop —or rather zoom ; he went from virtually the lowest commissioned rank to stand next door to a general. That, as I said before, was unique.

Do you know anything about music ? You do ? Well, you know how from *ppp* the music can rise to *fff* and then tail away again to *ppp*. That's how it was with Lawrence. He started as second " loot." That's *ppp*. Then he went suddenly up to full colonel—*fff*. And after the war, and of his own volition, reverted to aircraftsman, the lowest rank in the Air Force. That's *ppp* again—in fact, *pppp* !

CRASHES : AS DONE AT ABOUKIR

The particularly dreadful mess on the tarmac (bottom right) is from where the last of the "Apple-snatchers" left for the cemetery.

But to come back to our own story. We left Aurans, very much the Arab, leaning against a wall on the railway platform at Ismailia. To him came again the A.D.C. whom he had questioned as to the identity of the general.

" General Allenby would like to see you," he reported, " in the waiting-room."

That must have been a happy interview for both of them. Allenby had heard of Lawrence, and of what he had done with, and for, Feisal. And Lawrence learned that here was a Brass Hat who not only was personally and tangibly interested in his, Lawrence's, endeavours, but was also prepared to back them for, and on behalf of, the British Government. That interview changed the whole face of the campaign in the East. Thenceforward, Feisal and Allenby were not only allies, but allies working together.

At first the official British aid was not exactly a hundred per cent. British in quality. For instance, the first batch of 60,000 rifles was more dangerous to the pro-British Arabs than to the enemy. They were Japanese-made " relics " of the Russo-Japanese war, and though the calibre was correct, the barrels were not meant for the modern ammunition that was supplied with them. However, there were no such defects in the big bags of English sovereigns that went to Feisal for provisioning and paying his fighting men. And, as time went on, the British support became more and more comprehensive.

Now to return to Feisal. By 27 June, 1916, he had occupied Yanbo. Maybe you have read of this

G

historical port. In 24 B.C. Augustus Caesar sent 11,000 picked Roman soldiers to Yanbo, as a base for an attack on Arabia. After six unhappy months in the desert, a sorry remnant returned to Yanbo and sailed for Egypt. The enterprise had failed. They had learned what Lawrence already knew when he rejoined Feisal at Yanbo—that an army warring in Arabia must be able to endure much, while living on practically nothing. That he had truly learned this lesson was soon proved. He pushed on to El Wejh, about 120 miles to the north, and traversed that waterless desert without the loss of a single man. In addition to this, he forced the Turkish garrison to surrender.

Other Arab raids were taking place, in other parts of the country. I shall not go into full details, but you must know that Feisal took Akaba, a Turkish base of immense tactical value. On the strength of this, Lawrence was able to borrow twenty machine-guns from the navy.

(Some months after the war, by the way, Lawrence was asked by the navy to return the guns. He was very sorry, but he could not do so, he replied—he had mislaid them !)

With these Arab successes, culminating in the fall of Akaba, the Turkish and German " heads " were not a little bothered. Obviously, some unusual and very strategical mind was behind the whole business. The tactics employed were far more serious than the usual Arab hit-loot-and-run stunt ; under these latter circumstances a one-tribe war soon ended when the lords and masters of Arabia took the field.

There were investigations, and Lawrence's " place in the sun " was discovered.

It was obviously useless for the Turks to try to apprehend this British interloper. So the enemy tried a scheme that in the past had been most successful in dealing with troublesome people. They set a price on his head—£5000. Aurans (his sherifian title and his friendship with Feisal notwithstanding) was still an infidel trespassing on sacred soil. And £5000 was a tremendous sum in Arab eyes. As a matter of fact the reward was increased to £10,000. It goes to show the tremendous prestige of Lawrence, that this offer found no takers from the hundreds of thousands of tribesmen with whom the big-little Englishman was in personal contact.

From my experience of the Arabs I am quite sure that there were many who would have liked to earn that blood-money ; and that some Britishers even would have been stabbed, or shot, for it. But those extraordinary blue eyes, and the high esteem accorded their owner by Feisal, must have been a protection far more potent than Lawrence's personal prowess. For blue eyes terrified the Arabs—blue eyes were far more potent than the " evil eye." Lawrence often proved it. One afflicted with the evil eye would be brought into his presence, and Aurans, after staring at him for some minutes, would declare that, by the grace of Allah, the evil spell had been driven off. And the ex-evil-eyed one, and the spectators, would be convinced that Allah had indeed been good.

After the fall of Akaba, tribes flocked to Lawrence. They included the best fighting men in
Arabia. And each time Lawrence went to Palestine
to see Allenby, the degree of co-operation increased
between the British and the Arab forces ; and increasing support—money, stores, munitions, and so
forth—was available to the latter. At this time,
particularly, the Arab forces were worthy of culti-
vation. They were 200,000 strong. Although
the Lawrence plan did provide for some degree of
British order, they were not trained along what is
euphemistically called " civilized " lines. But
fighting was as normal a work-a-day happening
for them as it was for a Tommy to shave.

The Feisal-Lawrence attack on El Hasa was one
of their most ambitious and important actions.   I
want to tell you of it, because it shows yet another
side to Lawrence's character.   It was a battle of
fluctuating fortunes, Lawrence triumphing over all
reverses until a squadron of German Albatroses
swooped down from the skies.   Their appearance,
and their hail of bullets and bombs, were too much
for the Arabs.   They retreated, and with them
went Lawrence.   But not because he was scared—
Lawrence did not know the meaning of fear.

He retreated because he wanted to get the range
accurately.   So he calmly paced off the yards until
he gave the artillery the word to fire.   The Arabs,
by then, had two Egyptian-manned mountain guns.
The gun-fire was devastating.   The line occupied
by the Turks was on flintlike rock, and the richochet-
ting splinters and shrapnel caused as many casualties

as the direct hits did. Such obvious and gratifying results stayed the Arab retirement. Then Lawrence cut loose with his Hotchkiss and Vickers guns. Finish for Jacko ! The survivors were chased into Hasa Valley.

That was typical of the military campaign, and its success was born of Lawrence's genius. Nor was he merely a strategist, a master-mind pushing the puppets hither and thither from a kind of control-point behind the scenes of action. No. At every opportunity he joined in the scrap himself. And he certainly had proof there was a war on. He was wounded on no fewer than twenty occasions. But such was the toughness and fortitude of the man that never once did he report sick—or whatever the Arab equivalent of that is. He used to bear his reconditioning either on the march or in a bivouac.

Lawrence had an unshakable belief in the healing-powers of nature. This lady was his doctor-in-chief. Besides, as I said before, the Arabs were an exceptionally hardy people, who made light of wounds. Aurans, living Arab, had to show Arab fortitude.

While on the subject of war injuries: Lawrence also had more than a fair share of luck, so far as aircraft were concerned. He was in five crashes. One of these occurred in Italy when he was being flown to England. There were four in the plane. Lawrence was the only survivor. Yet, when he voluntarily forwent his war rank after the war, it was the Royal Air Force he joined, after a short stay in the Tank Corps. What had happened, and what might happen——that line of reasoning obviously did not affect Lawrence.

Back to Arabia, to Lawrence, and now to his favourite personal exploit, train-wrecking. At first he wrecked mainly to procure supplies. A start was made near Maan, on the Aleppo-Mecca line between Deraa and Medina, where 3000 Turks were garrisoned. The Arabs knew nothing of mine-laying——nor did Lawrence for that matter. But he was a quick learner. He had studied under a Royal Engineers officer at Yanbo. He had learned that if you treated 'em kindly, dynamite fuses and the like would eat out of your hand. He also learned that it would not be wise to pass on his knowledge of high explosives to Arabs. Not because they could not be trusted, but because the Arab, brave fellow that he was, was not quite as careful as he might be in the matter of firing fuses.

So, perforce, Lawrence played a lone hand. He succeeded in his first attempt. He had a most interested audience of Arabs on the summit of the nearest hill. Once the mine was blown up——under the engine——the Arabs joined in the fun. The train was scuppered. Then the raiders left——for parts unknown.

One of the most interesting phases of these min-ing exploits was that, so far as supply-trains were concerned, Lawrence only aimed to hold up the train——not to destroy either it or the line. While the train, and the line, were only being temporarily disabled, he knew that trains and supplies would continue to come along the railway. And he wanted it that way. Like the Scarlet Pimpernel, he would pop up at the least expected times, and in the most unexpected places. He had inside knowledge about Turkish railroad movement ; and he blew up so many trains, or rather parts of them, that the casualties among the rolling stock necessitated drastic reductions in the services. Seats in far back Aleppo or Damascus sold for five or six times the normal price. But the people who paid these fancy prices stipulated that the seats must be in the rear carriages.

Remember how the Red Indians used to scalp their victims, and thus provide proof-positive of their victory? Well, Lawrence had a similar scheme with regard to his railway victories—he used to " souvenir " the number-plates from the engine. Then he added other " scalps " to the collection—platform bells and mile-posts. The bells came from the railway stations along the Hejaz line. They used to be rung to warn passengers that the train was about to start. Lawrence took them in his stride, as it were. And also the mile-posts from along the track.

Characteristically, after the war, he distributed his loot among his friends.

This planting of " tulips "—that was Lawrence's name for the mines—was a most hazardous undertaking. Especially when the Turk got to know that Lawrence was on the job—Lawrence with his £10,000 head. But only on one occasion was he taken unawares. That was when he blew up the engine of a " supply-train " that proved to be a troop-train. When the smoke from the explosion cleared away, the entrained troops saw a solitary figure on a nearby knoll, and set out for him—and the £10,000—at the run. As usual, Lawrence had himself fired the mine, and his men were farther away from the line, hiding behind the rocks. The Turks reached Lawrence first, or rather practically reached him. But he whipped out his long-barrelled Colt and put in some deadly work. The Arabs finished it. That train carried many sacks of Turkish silver coin and notes.

Before the campaign was over, Lawrence had seventy-nine " tulip " raids to his credit. And the story goes that he proposed to make it an even total by planting a few " tulips " under British H.Q. in Cairo!

Another occasion when Lawrence was still closer to serious trouble was when he had gone raiding in an armoured car. That was in September 1918. The objective was the German aerodrome at Deraa. The Germans were not altogether caught napping, and their machine-gun fire was so accurate that bullets entered the driver's slit in the armour and tore the knuckles off Lawrence's hand. But he carried on, and shot up a number of German machines on the ground before he turned for home.

Those of the Huns who could take off in their planes did so, and two of them tried to bomb Lawrence's car. Almost, they scored a direct hit—a bomb blew off a tyre. But Lawrence and his armoured car got home.

Lawrence was supremely self-confident. His exploits prove this. But he never thought himself infallible. For instance, he knew the country better than any one else on our side, and he had his own channels of information, but he always sought first-hand knowledge of the " doings " when an action impended. Again, he knew that when it came to reports, the accuracy of his own Arabs was not above reproach ; they had a bad habit of exaggerating, and their knowledge of military engineering, topography and the like was, to put it mildly, limited. So when his Arabs began to move north from Akaba in the direction of Azrak, Lawrence often asked for air reconnaissance of the Turkish strong-points ahead. The Turkish garrisons were small but mobile. They used to keep an eye on the railway to ensure safe working conditions for the trains. These strong-points were an unknown quantity. Lawrence wanted definite and authentic information about them.

Come along with me on one of these recos. I admit frankly that we of No. 1 Squadron were not keen about these jobs. Too lonely. Too far off the beaten track. True, there was no Archie, and very rarely did a Hun show up in the sky. But down below was what I will call, for want of a better term, unpleasant mystery. We knew there were people there—hostile Arabs, Circassians, or Turks. What they would do to one in the event of a forced landing was only a matter of conjecture and. . . . But—this is our job, as set out in the following order :

To-morrow morning, 6 July, 1918, a special reco. ordered by G.H.Q. on behalf of the Arabs, will reconnoitre Derwish-Aneiza and Maan, all these places are on the Hejaz Railway and about 90 miles south of Amman.

And here are the individual instructions :

Brigade request reconnaissance of defences in and around Derwish-Aneiza-Maan. 6th inst. Escort of 1 machine considered adequate. Height of reconnaissance not specified. Time 0900 hours. Report Centre—17 miles due E. of Bir-el-Shedia at 1200 hours. Reconnoitring machine will drop copy of reconnaissance on Report Centre after usual identification procedure has been carried out. (Two green and one white light from machine answered by two reds from ground.) Every endeavour must be made by officers conducting reconnaissance to convey to our Allies, the Arabs, a thorough appreciation of the strength and dispositions of the enemy in and around the areas aforementioned.

1st Squadron will make such refuelling arrangements as may be necessary in order to effect the above.

MAP. Sheet MAAN. Ottoman Empire $\frac{1}{500,000}$

Acknowledge.
Ends.

40 Wing 5/7/18.
T. C. MACAULEY, Staff Captain.

Sounds very simple.   But let us have a look at the
map and roughly plot out our course.   Well, there's
one thing about it—their report centre shouldn't be
very hard to find.   Any one can pick up that huge
depression of El-Jafar from the air.   What is it,
you ask ?   Just a huge hole in the ground measuring
about seven miles long by one mile wide.   Some
fifteen wadys drain into it, that is when there is any
water to drain away.   Oh, yes, it rains sometimes
out there—perhaps twice or three times a year.   Let
us now put a pin-point in the map where the report
centre should be.   No, we will not mark it clearly.
You never know, we may be shot down, and a
marked map would be invaluable to the enemy.

In all, it looks as if the flight will be at least 360
miles in length without any extra " looks."

What is an extra " look " ?

Observers always confirm the information they
have gleaned from the ground.   Fly over it again.
That's an extra look.   As a rule, the pilots think this
procedure is unnecessary.   But that's because they
don't like the extra work.   Actually, the extra look
is most important.

Just a minute while I work out our fuellings.
Won't bother you with details.   But we shall have
to land twice so that we'll have full tanks for the
longest hops.   It's no use quoting Wiley Post,
Lindbergh, and Kingsford Smith.   Remember this
is eighteen years ago and 360 miles was far too
much for one hop in those days.   At least with a
" Brisfit."

What height is specified for our job of work ?

Um—" not specified." That means we can please ourselves. And, incidentally, this gives us scope to shoot up a stray Turk or two.

Let's see. . . . We have three hours allowed us to finish the reco. and drop the report. We'll do it. See you on the tarmac to-morrow morning. You'll find plenty of flying-kit in that cupboard in the hangar . . .

Ah! There you are! O.K. We'll squeeze you into the cockpit. Sit on that low seat—you'll be quite comfy. We are taking only about 600 rounds for our back guns—one twin Lewis. Oh, have a look in that rack and check up the Very lights. The colours, I mean. Good ! Now here's our escort machine—from " B " Flight. Off we go! The escort will fall in behind and slightly above us.

Now we're at 1500 feet. That's high enough to keep us cool this morning. We should make Beersheba in about thirty minutes. We're going to land on the old Hun aerodrome. Don't worry—the aerodrome is all right. All our bomb holes were filled up months ago.

Watch the country change from that black basalt formation you now see, to undulating hills covered with low scrub, or bushes ; then to patches of sand, more sand, and eventually all sand. Sand, as far as the eye can see in any direction. That's the desert. . . . Now here is Beersheba ahead. We'll land in a minute or two. Sit tight. . . . Well, that's that. There's our petrol.

Our next leg is to Derwish, where the job proper

commences. We'll fly about 6000 feet. Just high enough to cover the hills. Hop in. This time we're leaving all friends behind us, with the exception of the escorting Bristol.

Keep the map on your knees. Our course will take us about ten miles south of the Dead Sea. I'll keep an eye on the escort. Seems peculiar, doesn't it, flying over hostile territory and yet no front line, no Archies. But look down there to the south. See that small Arab encampment ? Well, if we forced-landed near them, our fate would be decided by the fact whether they were pro-British this week or pro-Turk. Funny blighters. Look ! There's the Dead Sea showing up now.

See ! Hell ! The escort has fired a white light. That means he has engine failure. Bad luck. Round he goes, heading back to Beersheba. Hope he'll get there all right. In any case, we've got our own job to do. But it is a hundred per cent. lonely, now. We should pick up the Hejaz Railway any time now. It is out in front. Those clouds may be a bit troublesome. I'll tell you more about clouds on the way back.

There's the railway now. See if you can pick up the station buildings at Derwish. There they are. I'll be pretty busy from now on. Keep one eye on the sky, will you ?

Not much at Derwish, anyhow. Now for Aneiza. We'll go straight down along the road. There are a few camels down there moving south.

Hello, someone is " pooping " off at us with a

machine-gun from the ground. No, you cannot see any smoke of discharge. But those angry bees whizzing by are bullets. Don't worry, we'll soon be clear of that. It's coming from the machine-gun emplacement in that trench north of the station. No reprisals. I've got about everything noted and we have to push on to Maan. We should see quite a number of Turkish patrols along the road and out east of the railway. There's a small one to start with. Evidently they fear another of Lawrence's " tulip " raids—no trains about.

There's Maan away in the distance to the south. Expect to find quite a garrison there. They've got at least two field-guns. Those bursts over there to the left tell the story. No, I can't see 'em. The guns I mean. But the Turks sometimes use that type of gun for anti-aircraft fire. Proves they haven't any pukka Archies. We will have to do five or six circuits here to enable me to get all the dope. Quite a big place, isn't it ? . . .

O.K. That's finished ! Now there's only this message-dropping business to be done. How's the time ? 11.33 hours ? Good. We'll fly N.E. for fifteen minutes and then cut down to the R.C.— that's short for report centre. Never do to fly direct to it—Jacko might make things nasty for our friends.

Hand me that Very pistol and two green cartridges and one white. In another minute or so we should be over the spot. No, it's no use looking for their identification sign. They won't put it out until they see and answer our lights. They are probably hiding in the rocks on the side of the wady. Well, here goes with the Verys. They should answer with two reds . . . two reds it is. There they are—over there to the left, off the road. Put this copy of the reco. in that message-bag, and throw it out when I tell you. I'll glide down to a hundred or so feet over them. There's their ground strip out now. See it—that white sheet about ten feet square with a red crescent in the centre Righto, let the bag go !—Good shot ! That tall Arab has picked it up. What's that ? Oh, that short figure in white ? Yes, he may be Lawrence. He seems to be taking things very calmly anyhow.

Now for home. Or, rather, Beersheba first. We'll want some more " juice."

Care to go up into the clouds ? They are now at about 9000 feet. Good. You'll find these great tumbled-up masses of snowy down intensely interesting. They are never still ; never retain any particular formation for any length of time. This country is noted for its clouds. We never have fogs here, and very little rain. So clouds here are more friendly than those on other fronts. If you're being pressed by a Hun or two, just nick into 'em and you have a refuge. It is darn difficult to ferret a plane out of cloud. And a mite dangerous. But it's great fun playing " follow my leader." That is when it's only a game.

Well, here we are. Home again. Hope you enjoyed the flip. And maybe you'd like to see a copy of the report we dropped. Here it is :

" A " FORM
MESSAGES AND SIGNALS

To COL. LAWRENCE,
 Arab Army,
  Report Centre L55.

Map Sheet Maan $\frac{1}{500,000}$

Derwish 2 B.T. (bell tents) 12 shelters 50 infantry near station series rifle pits NE. of station. Barbed wire on high ground E. and South of Station Stop Aneiza cav. [cavalry] patrol 1 mile N. of station on road. 1 Marquee 7 B.T. 38 shelters in camp 200 yards E. of station. Small reservoir broken line of trenches on high ground NE. SE. and S. of station, no wire visible 1 M.G. emplacement on NE. end of defences. No artillery or anti-aircraft weapons observed Stop 2 camel trains of 35 animals moving south along road 8 miles N. of Maan, no patrols seen Stop Maan two field guns firing at machine from apparently gun pits on road 500 yards south of railway siding. One train of engine 11 trucks and van in railway station. Engine with steam up facing north, large camp consisting of 35 B.T. 250 shelters on north side of road between town of Maan and railway station, series of redoubts cover Maan from the south and are astride Akaba road 2 miles south of railway elbow series of disconnected trenches run in a NE. direction on

OUR LAWRENCE

high ground from a point 3 miles due S. of railway station thence NE. to a point 1½ miles north of kilo 470. Small cav. camp on road just north of town no movement observed on road to south. Three large dumps in railway yard. Estimate of garrison under canvas 2500 all arms. Fired 300 rounds into camp, troops disappeared into funk holes around camp boundaries. No motor transport observed one horse transport park of 15 vehicles near station. No movement around station. Small piquets on all railway culverts 5 miles N. and 5 miles south of railway station. Flew low over town and Main camp but was not engaged by machine-gun fire, riflemen posted on high ground N. of camp fired at machine. Two reservoirs containing water one S. of town other north of railway station. No railway movement observed along railway as far south as kilo 520. Message ends.

Time, 1133 hours.
Visibility good.
Height, 5500 feet.
1st Squadron.

You'll notice I've set out that little affair we had with the camp. Sorry, I was sharp with you then. But a man cannot be conversational when he is blazing away at moving targets.

The most romantic Lawrence stories concern his spying expeditions behind the Turkish lines. His many disguises included that of a gipsy woman of Syria. But he abandoned that, after one unpleasant

H

experience—when some drunken Turkish soldiers tried to make love to him ! Towards the end of the campaign he invariably used British khaki as a disguise. Because, he explained, it was too brazen to be suspected. He would return with all kind of queer " loot "—uniforms, equipment, exploders, fuses, camel-trappings, camp-gear, and Zeiss glasses. And always with valuable military information.

Actually, his most daring stunt was carried through during a spare fortnight in 1918. There was nothing doing in particular; he was waiting for a band of his warriors to join him. So he went a roving. Disguised as a gipsy woman, mounted on a camel and accompanied by a Bedouin, he passed through the Turkish lines and went as far north as Palmyra. There, he hoped to find an influential Bedouin chief whom he wanted to win over to Feisal. The chief was away, and Lawrence rode on to Baalbeck, an ancient city whose ruined temples are one of the architectural wonders of the world. He went to Baalbeck to make sure that a tribe, whose chieftain was pro-Feisal, would be ready for action should Allenby make a general advance.

But before he made this investigation he painted what was surely the most crazily impudent portrait in the Lawrence gallery. Two miles from the city he dismounted, took off his Arab robes, to be revealed as a British officer. Thus clad, and solo, he swaggered in boldly. And this was 200 miles behind the Turkish lines ! The Turkish soldiers saluted, thinking him a German officer. Lawrence returned the salute, German fashion. Then he made a cursory survey of the fortifications, and, sublime act of impudence, set out to visit the Turkish military school where there were 1000 young officers in training. But when some older officers showed up ahead Lawrence casually walked the other way—back to his camel, his disguise, and the camp of the friendly Bedouins.

There he revealed his identity. Imagine the stimulating effect on his hosts of so extraordinary a visitation. Here was the great man in person—he had come 200 miles through, and behind the enemy lines, to visit them. And he could speak their tongue ! So impressed were they that they clamoured for an immediate Syrian revolt. No, the time was not yet ripe, explained Lawrence. But since they demanded action, action he would give them. Afterwards he described the resultant stunt as a " picture show."

That night he took a party of the tribesmen down along the Aleppo-Beirut railway line behind Baalbeck, to one of the biggest bridges in the Near East. There he planted " tulips " at both ends—by the way he had to " borrow " the dynamite from a Turkish engineer dump—connected them up, and carried the electric connections to the top of a nearby hill, where, at his invitation, the tribesmen gathered. This was the " grandstand." Lawrence, or should I say Sherif Aurans, touched the switch, and the bridge was a wreck. Whereupon the tribesmen swore oaths by Allah they would join Hussein and his Faithful.

On another of his visits to Turkish territory he

went to Damascus.   He was in British uniform, and mounted on a camel.   Outside a café he saw a notice with his picture at the top, offering £5000 reward for the capture, dead or alive, of " El Orans, Destroyer of Railways."   His reaction ? He dismounted, seated himself near the notice, ordered coffee, spent a leisurely hour over it, and then went away.   Only when you heard him tell the story could you understand how much he enjoyed the experience. . . . There's no accounting for tastes.

I have already mentioned that the Turks had used Akaba as a base.   When the Arabs took it Lawrence put it to the same use.   A very handy place, for most of his supplies came up to it per the British Fleet, and Admiral Wemyss was a very good friend.   Like Allenby, Wemyss did not take long to realize the value of Lawrence's work.   With the aid of these two big men Lawrence secured an armoured car section, a few mountain guns, and some obsolete British aeroplanes.   The latter formed what was known in official circles as " X " Flight, commanded by Major Ross.   One of the two other officers was Captain Junor, a very gallant R.F.C. officer.

In those days, the Turks and Germans would not allow that kind of thing.   I mean, something had to be done about an Arab force having an aircraft auxiliary.   Soon German machines appeared on the scene, and the Arabs developed acres of goose-flesh.   If there is one thing the Arabs like less than a bomb-dropping enemy machine, it is two enemy

A SQUADRON OF LAWRENCE'S REGULAR IRREGULARS

The horses are magnificent Arab thoroughbreds.

machines dropping more bombs—and dropping 'em on the Faithful. Nor did the Huns content themselves with bombing Akaba, its troops and etceteras. No. They followed the Arab force as it moved north—more and more Huns, with more and more bombs. One morning eight Huns came over in a bunch.

" *Tiara, tiara,*" yelled the Arabs. *Tiara* was their word for plane.

But all was not lost. Snorting fire and brimstone from all her aged pores, a decrepit B.E. dashed aloft to repel the aerial marauders. She made such a determined fuss and flurry that the superior Hun machines were driven off. But only temporarily. The homing B.E. prefaced their return, and there were three irate Huns on her tail. The pilot of the B.E. (Junor of the R.F.C) made violent gestures, which told Lawrence that he, Junor, was out of petrol, and was going to land immediately, if not sooner. He landed. And at that very moment one of the Huns did a masterly job of work—he scored a direct hit on the B.E. with a bomb. But fortune favours the brave. When the smoke cleared away a very dishevelled pilot crawled out from the wreck. He was uninjured.

That bomb wrote " finis " to Lawrence's last B.E.

Next time Lawrence visited Allenby he asked for modern aeroplanes. Allenby " came to light." That was when our squadron came actively into the picture. Previously our Bristols had only been used to " ferry " Lawrence to and fro between his " herd " and G.H.Q. (Richon). One of the first machines to be attached to " T.E." was a Bristol Fighter ; its pilot, Lieutenant Arthur Murphy—" Spud " to us. He had to do something about those morning raids. Two Huns used to come over regularly and, with bombs and guns, make things uncomfortable for the Arabs.

There is nothing like meeting trouble half-way, so Spud went up to meet the visitors before they arrived. But the enemy equivalent of our bush wireless was busy in those days. The raiders failed to appear. Some days later Spud ran into one or two Huns more than he could cope with. He was shot down out on the desert. Neither he nor his observer was injured, but the plane was very much the worse for Hun attentions. Three of the four longerons were shot through, and at least fifty bullets had struck the machine. A bad state of affairs. Desert, hundreds of miles from anywhere, very little water or food and a machine that, so far as flying was concerned, just did not exist.

But Spud was an engineer, with grit and initiative. The only metal available was the camera stand. That had to do. Tools ? Only those in the roll, and they were for engine repairs, not for major aircraft reconstruction jobs. However, Spud did it. He made three complete sets of ligatures, which he bolted and bound round the damaged longerons. Then he took a wire off here and there and connected it up in such a way as to reduce the strain on the damaged parts, and flew the wreck 180 miles to Ramleh. That was a classic feat. At least we chaps of the squadron thought so.

Other machines and pilots of No. 1 Squadron were posted to the Lawrence " Air Force."

It may be amusing to you to know that we should not have been nearly so welcome to the Arabs as we were, had it not been for a serious nuisance we encountered at Azrak on the Amman-Baghdad route, and which induced us to change our dress. The nuisance was a very vicious fly, about the size of the Egyptian " canary " (blowfly), which attacked the exposed parts of the body, and drew blood. At first we used to wear flying-kit as a defence, but it was then summer, and the prevention was just as uncomfortable as the trouble itself. Finally, we adopted the Arab head-dress. The Arab has no love for the infidel, especially when said infidel stands on holy ground. But this Arab head-dress served more or less as a pass.

Until the Bristols arrived on the scene, most of the Arabs had never seen an aeroplane on the ground. More often than not, the machines they saw in the air were German, and decidedly unfriendly. When the first of our machines came amongst them, the Bedouins punched and pinched the crews. Not with malice, but to make sure the people inside the flying-togs were really and truly human beings.

When the Lawrence force was at Azrak, the nearest German aerodrome was at Deraa, a few miles to the north-west. So extraordinarily clear was the atmosphere that from the Arab advanced landing-ground it was quite possible to hear the enemy revving up their engines. This served splendidly as an alarm and enabled our chaps to meet the Hun half-way.

As Ross Smith was one of the Lawrence pilots it was not long before the Deraa Huns preferred to fly in directions other than towards Azrak. But there were some scraps. In one of them two of our Bristols got entangled with a formation of five Huns. Two of the latter bit the dust and another was chased home.

The Arabs liked to see our machines always in the air. They thought that then, and only then, would they be immune from German air attacks. But fuel was becoming a very serious problem. Petrol and oil had to be brought up hundreds of miles on the backs of " ships of the desert." And these " ships " were not " tankers."

The giant Handley-Page was requisitioned as a supply-ship—the one and only H.P. on the Eastern Front ; and, as befitted so important a weapon, it was on the " strength " of our squadron. Ross Smith was the pilot. To assuage the thirst of the Lawrence-attached Bristols, it was filled to the brim with tins of petrol, a ton in all, oil and spares ; and flown to Azrak. Lawrence was being driven along out there—in Feisal's car—when, twenty miles out, he met a very excited Arab. " The biggest *tiara* in the world," he yelled happily with uplifted arms. At Azrak, Lawrence and Co. found the Handley surrounded by a milling mob of exulting Arabs, popping off their rifles and shouting :

" At last Allah has sent us the aeroplane of which these others are foals." The glad tidings spread throughout the Hauran and across the Druse Mountains ; and the Arabs realized that they were on the winning side.

Next morning Lawrence was having breakfast with our fellows when a guard yelled " aeroplane up ! " The pilots sprinted to their Bristols, and took off. Five minutes later they were back at breakfast, having driven down a two-seater and put to flight three scouts. The sausages were still sizzling, and were treated as sausages should be treated after a successful scrap. The pilots were just topping off with grapes, when again the guard yelled " aeroplanes ! " No Drake touch—no stopping and finishing the game. Action. This time a scout was brought down in flames.

When working in with Allenby's operations, one of Lawrence's greatest problems was communication. Wireless, that is military W/T, did not then have a sufficient range. Nor could aeroplanes be spared to run a daily D.R.L.S. (Dispatch Rider Letter Service).

So the army pigeon service was called upon. We were not optimistic. How would the birds react to the unusual desert conditions ? Would the service be available when required ? And what of the Arabs ?—adroit thieves and keen marksmen who are inordinately fond of game of any description. How would the pigeons fare at their hands ? Well, one morning a crate of pigeons arrived at the squadron, and we received instructions as to their training. Single birds were to be taken out in the machines and released from varying distances and at different heights, and a very careful log was to be kept of the performance of each bird.

One of them we called " Jenny." She soon became the pet of the squadron and was most carefully guarded in training. She had a sort of net for carriage in the machines. When the time came for the bird to be dispatched, the net would be lifted and the bird thrown up and back, down the slipstream. The first solo must have been a very thrilling experience for the bird. But once out Jenny would stick to the machine until she had sorted herself out, and then how she would streak for home !

But the pigeon problem did not finish when the training was over. It was simple to deliver the birds to Lawrence at Azrak, but what of it when he moved ? We got this necessary mobility by building small cane cages, with a kind of cell or compartment for each bird, and a parachute for the cages. So when the birds were to be delivered from aloft to the ground, we simply tossed the cages overboard, and the parachute did the rest.

The scheme was most successful. Even though they had to cover distances up to 300 miles, and over the worst type of inhospitable country, Jenny and her girl friends always got their messages through. So far as we could ascertain, not one pigeon was lost or killed in action. But there were casualties—pigeon pie was a welcome addition to the menu. And . . . er . . . by the way, silk parachutes can be converted into excellent pyjamas and shirts.

Came a time when our happy, inspiring relations with Lawrence were broken off. Back to No. 1 Squadron we went with our Bristols, our Handley-Page, our pigeons, and our pigeon-gear. This was when Allenby's advance was developing, and there was other and more urgent work for No. 1 Squadron. Nor was it holiday-time for Lawrence. His force had to cover an area so wide that at times the columns were hundreds of miles apart. Lawrence had to rely on Allenby to keep him in touch with the general development of the offensive, by means of machines dropping messages on pre-selected report centres. And so we lost close touch with Lawrence. But we who flew with and for him remember him with affectionate respect. He was so very much a big man, was little Lawrence.

Even now, with the flood of information that was loosed after his death, the real reason why he joined the Royal Air Force with the lowest rank, and never moved therefrom, is not authoritatively known. But I'll bet my royalties to a pinch of salt that all our officers who met Aircraftsman " Shaw " sprang to attention and addressed him as " sir."

I wonder whether he will use any " tulips " where he has gone ?

CHAPTER VI

" CAM "

You know the song which tells how the " Admiral told the captain and the captain told . . . " ? Well, it was something like that at Belah, when No. 67 Squadron of 40th Wing, R.F.C., was there in 1917. Someone would rush into the mess and shout, " Cam's coming in," and the news would fly from mess to hangar, from hangar to workshop, and from workshop to quarters, so that by the time Cam and his 2.e were over the aerodrome every disengaged hand of the wing was a spectator. For Cam and a 2.e were one of the brightest spots of entertainment. Almost it could be termed :

" Landings—as done by a horsebreaker."

When Cam joined the squadron, a whisper went round that he could not land 2.e's, and after the first exhibition had verified the news, the wing was always ready for more.

Well. The machine would make its approach, engine off, of course, and we'd hear Cam roaring at his mount : " Hop, you so-and-so. Just one more —a little engine, please—whoa, you such-and-such, this ain't a (generally speaking) buck-jumping contest." And he'd land. A perfect landing— but for the fact that it was 50 feet above the aerodrome.

" CAM "

(The " rascal " is sixth from the left in upper picture and second from the left in the lower one.)

On goes the engine, and off goes the machine for another attempt. That was only Act 1. A good time is being had by all, senior officers included. That is, by all on the ground. Cam, poor fellow, is not so happy.

Over comes the 2.e again. And once more we see a fine aeroplane struggling to put herself down, and her pilot—unintentionally, of course—doing everything possible to prevent her. As failure follows failure, Cam gets more and more perplexed ; more and more verbal. And we await the curtain-fall of Act 2. No, not a crash, but the last desperate resort of the harassed pilot. We would be howling with glee by this time, and when, with a fierce movement, Cam would pull off his long muffler, even our legs would get laughter-shaken, for we knew what was to follow. Cam would add direct violence to tongue-lashing. He would ride that plane. He would master it. Flailing the muffler, whip-wise, along the fuselage, he would ride the " bus " in. " I'll show yer, yer this-and-that which-and-what. I'll learn yer to pig-root. . . . Take that, and that." And the " whip " would lash the " flanks " of the long-suffering plane. Ordinary humane methods having failed, by brute strength he would master his mount. But, oh, those landings ! Those bumps ! Those hops—and hops !

Act 3 of the comedy would open at the hangar, after Cam had taxied there. The C.O. speaking :

" Well, you're not showing much progress with your landings."

Cam leans against the nearest machine, bench,

post, girder, or trestle—he was the type that had to lean.

" Stand to attention, man ! "

" Sorry, sir." Cam slumps again.

" But don't you think my second landing in the last attempt was the best of the five ? " meekly asks Cam. (His landings usually consisted of at least five hops.)

C.O. trying to control his face, and at the same time retain official dignity : " You . . . er . . . must make an . . . an attempt to . . . er . . . master your landings, my man."

Then Cam would really straighten his shoulders, and flare :

" Attempt be damned ! What d'yer think I've been doing for the last week ? " And before the C.O. could reply : " But sir, I'll take the sting out of the what-you-please even if I've got to put a flank rope on her ! " Then he'd smile. And when Cam smiled, even C.O.s forgot rules and regulations, and ham-handed landings.

Between you, me, and the lamp-post, we Flying Corps wallahs liked ourselves. We were spared a lot of the rotten routine jobs that the other branches of the service had to put up with. No guards, no stables, no stand-to, no minute-to-go-for-zero. Our uniforms were cut so as to set off our distinctive manliness and beauty. Oh yes, we were manly and good to the eye—ask the nicest girls in Alexandria and Cairo. And war flying was great work—if you didn't weaken.

We of the No. 67 Squadron particularly liked

ourselves, especially when we saw the droves of applicants for transfers to our corps. And these applicants were coming from splendid types of chaps who made up the Anzac, and the Australian Mounted Divisions. At times it almost seemed as if there were nearly two divisions of would-be pilots waiting on our squadron doorstep.

It was not the smart, well-turned-out man who was chosen, however. No, the examiners chose rather the crack horsemen, and the musicians—the men with the hands. And, of course, the crack rifle-shots had a big pull. Not so much because of their marksmanship, but because they had eyes— the kind of eye that goes to make a good pilot.

Fitness was a point in an applicant's favour. Not a fitness brought about by hard work and hard rations, but the fitness developed by sports, like tennis and swimming and cricket—sports which develop co-ordination of brain and limb, as well as good wind and the right kind of muscle.

In one way and another, we had as fine a body of men seeking to join us as you would have found on any front. Probably I have no right to say that—I was only in the East. Anyway, believe you me, they were a bonny lot. More often than not, the examining officer was just as sorry to reject the applicant as the applicant was to get " No ! "

Cam came and was chosen, at the time when the applications were at flood-peak. So he was " the goods." But even his best cobber would never have backed him to win a beauty or a deportment competition. With his nondescript features, and

wretched slouchy carriage, he seemed to consist of
liquid waiting to be poured into a saddle. That
was the point—Cam was a horseman. He was
born and bred in outback Queensland. There were
some great horsemen in those Australian divisions,
but Cam was generally accorded to be one of the
best. And when he stripped, that lean lathy build
of his told of a bush horseman's strength.

Well, we soon got to know him when he joined
the squadron. He got his " brevvy " at No. 22
Training Squadron, Aboukir—as a two-seater pilot,
flying 2.e's. This was a Tommy unit, and, as we
learned subsequently, Cam was of the average run
of trainees. He did the usual twenty to thirty hours
of dual and solo that was sufficient to turn out a
war pilot in those days ; and came to us without
" red ink " on his confidential report. By the way,
this confidential report was a pilot's shadow. Telling all the good and bad things officially known
about the subject, it followed him everywhere—
but out of the reach of the subject's hands.

Cam was incorrigible. His language was the
most pungent ; his imagery red-raw. But there
was something inherently clean about the man that
enabled him to get away with verbal murder. In
those hot, desert days, off-duty appearance was not
important. Shorts, a slouch hat, and a shirt were
sufficient for most occasions. But even with this
latitude Cam always managed to look slummocky
—always he was a blot on the squadron's sartorial
landscape. Yet he always wore a clean shirt.
How, we soon learned to our sorrow. He was an

" PARD "

(Flight-Lieutenant E. A. Mustard, D.F.C.) in full war paint. He has
lost a *d* in his name and grown a moustache since this photo was taken.

incorrigible " borrower." He could never see a clean shirt without " borrowing " it. When taxed with the crime, he had such drolly ingenious excuses that it was almost a pleasure to be a victim.

Not so with regard to his practical jokes. He was irrepressible—the scamp of the mess. Tents would collapse in the night ; officers would be summoned by phone to report to so-and-so at the most inconvenient times, and from the most inconvenient places ; petrol or soap would desecrate the soup on important mess nights ; guy-ropes would eventuate unexpectedly in one's path. And there was the classic downfall of Dr. X. Doc was very large and methodical. One early morn, a " bush telegram " went the rounds, and when Doc, in pyjamas, went his regular way—regularity is any doctor's watchword—every tent within eye range had its quota of spectators. Well, to make a short and rather low story still shorter and some six feet lower, the Doc crashed through the community seating accommodation, which someone had sawn almost through, into the deep trench beneath. An unhygienic episode. Cam escaped with the Scotch verdict—" not proven."

One of the things that used to mystify us, before we got to know the human gold that was Cam, was the instant popularity he used to win with Tommies —even those of the most exalted rank, social status, and wealth. Allenby, General " Biffy " Borton (our Wing C.O.), Captain Barnado—all of them really liked our pet rough-diamond. We know that, so far as language was concerned, he was the same to

the Brassiest Hats as he was to us. We knew that
he slouched in the most august presence ; that thus
situated the dear old cuss would whisk away imagin-
ary flies with his hat—he would never wear the more
impressive cap—and that his salutes had as much
snap in them as wet toast.

But it was not until after a very " posh " dinner
at Wing that we learned where Cam stood with the
English *élite*. Cam comes into our mess, grinning
broadly, and waving an invitation :

" Hey, what's the strength of this, Cappo ? " he
asks his Flight Commander.

" Damned if I now," replied " Cappo " ; " probably they require a *pilot* to fly His Nibs (Allenby)
up and down the line."

Cam agrees that this is likely and the flight wants
to know what Cam is going to do about it.

" Go, of course," chuckles Cam. " An order's
an order, isn't it ? Um', hope I have a clean shirt."

" You'll get a clean shirt all right," says his
Flight Commander, and reflectively, " Which reminds me I'd better go and lock my box now."

But for all the excitement, Cam turned out for
squadron parade the next morning in his usual nondescript attire : khaki shirt, shorts held up by a
web-equipment belt, tan shoes that lacked elbow-
grease, and his old slouch hat. As the day wore on
we, like Alice, got curiouser and curiouser as to how
the scamp would array himself. We knew he had
to be at Wing by 6.30 ; and we knew that, for all
his notorious unpunctuality, he would be there on
time—because cocktails were always " on tap " for

the guests prior to the serious business of the evening.

Well, all the squadron officers are casually (and not so casually) loitering near Cam's tent when he emerges at 6 pip emma and starts on his way to the waiting car. Consternation ! He is wearing a tunic, but no Sam Brown belt ; no hat. And, the age of miracles not being altogether past, his hair has been brushed ! Other than that, his attire is exactly the same as on the first parade of the day. We knew the futility of proffering advice. In any case we enjoyed the thought that, in this rig, the dear old sinner would be refused admission to such a meticulous mess. But the night wore on, and Cam did not return. Not until the small hours, when we were awakened by a cursing rumpus. Cam was voicing his views on the this-and-thats and so-forths who had turned his adjectival tent round. He was very drunk. Probably only his bushman's instinct had got him home.

When some of our lads went over to Wing the next morning, we got the good oil about Cam's début in their mess. It appears that Cam's weird attire had caused no trouble—in fact Wing expected it. Everything went well until two of the guests began what developed into an argument as to whether England or the Argentine produced the better horses. The arguers were a general and a millionaire captain (Captain Barnado can tell you who the latter was). Cam was obviously interested. He listened intently, patiently. Then he began to fidget. Finally he could not contain himself :

" England be b-gg-r-d ! " he roared suddenly, lifting himself out of his chair and pounding the table. " You poor bloody fools never saw a horse or a horseman until we blokes landed in this land of sand, sore eyes, and syphilis ! " Deathly silence. Cam sat down, looking abashed. Then a gale of laughter swept the mess. Everyone howled. Except Cam, who looked dumbfounded. Finally the C.O. arose and said :

" Gentlemen, I, we, owe our Australian guest an apology. Cam " (and here the C.O. turned towards him) " I wish to confess to being a conspirator. My guests wished me to support my boast as to your grip of er . . . descriptive English. That . . . er . . . debate you listened to so patiently was stage-managed. And your . . . er . . . comments concerning the views expressed bear out my boast in its entirety. Cam, I sincerely thank you."

After that it was straight sailing. Cam was at his ease. In that funny little voice of his, he sang them bush songs, recited " Banjo " Paterson as only a bushman can, and was generally the big entertainment of a big night.

Like his brother officers, Cam took a keen interest in the squadron's two mascots, " Mick " and " Charlie " ; mongrel dogs both. Mick was mostly terrier and he had a coat of long white hair. Also he was a flea-incubator. But so long as he kept his fleas to himself no one objected. However, Mick had a weakness for soft beds and he would take his afternoon siesta thereon. All sorts of remedies had been tried to keep the strength of Mick's army down to reasonable proportions, but none had proved of lasting efficacy.

One afternoon Cam came into his tent. He was dog-tired after a long and hectic job aloft. And just as he was about to slump on to his stretcher, he espied Mick in possession, lying on one of Cam's proudest possessions—a bed-cover. Cam hurled a shoe at Mick, and the latter hurriedly departed, leaving a lot of his "boarders" behind. Cam settled down to "shut-eye," but what with the heat and the fleas, sleep was impossible. His "dog-tiredness" increased in all directions! "Mick, you ——, you'll pay for this," we heard him roaring suddenly, and he was still cursing when at tea-time he came into the mess tent, flourishing a great pair of tailor's scissors. How he came by them was a mystery. We were getting philosophical about Cam's mysteries ; so did not question him about the scissors. Besides, he was advancing on Mick, and Mick was not awaiting the approach. However, Cam was not a bushman for nothing ; he soon cornered and captured Mick.

"Hold him, Bert, I'll fix those —— fleas once and for all." Cam must have imagined himself back in the shearing-shed, for when he had finished with the scissors, Mick had parted with all his "fleece"—even his eyebrows. Of course, the fleas went with the fleece. Mick looked as if he would have liked to be able to say "Thank you !"

Cam wouldn't or couldn't hurry. He just slouched along. Even when he was stand-by pilot and a Hun alarm sounded, he was his usual unhurried self. So to make the best of a bad job we used to have everything ready for him. Engine running, observer in his seat, and Cam's Sidcot suit and helmet awaiting him in his cockpit. Cam would saunter up, climb into his seat, and, without waiting to don his flying togs, take off. Once clear of the ground, he'd wriggle a foot and leg into the Sidcot, and if the jar on the rudder-bar caused the machine to lurch— it usually did—he'd talk, horse-breaker fashion, to the plane. Into the other leg ; observer leans forward and helps to hitch up the " strides " end of the suit, and, by the time 3000 feet had been climbed Cam was clad reasonably like a pilot.

And could that fellow moan ! The Wailing Wall at Jerusalem was a cabaret compared to his never-ending plaints. One day it would be no mail. Next day, no beer in the mess. Then no money. Or too wet, or too dry. Or no culture, or too much. Or too much flying, or not enough. But it did not take us long to realize that Cam was not letting off steam, or easing his liver. No, he was looking for a " bite." And woe betide the innocent who supplied it. For this untravelled " bushie," with no culture or anything of that kind, was never stuck for a retort. The beauty of it was that Cam never sought these verbal encounters so that he could be smart, and score. It was just fun.

If Cam had ever opened that big heart of his, I am sure we would have learned that the real reason for all his pranks was because he wanted to buck us up, make us laugh, take our thoughts from war.

Yes, I'm sure Cam had appointed himself squadron jester.

One of the very few things he did in the mess that was not born in laughter was whisky poker. This was at Ramleh. Before this, we used to trickle along to the mess at eleven every morning and have a few spots. Take it in turn to shout, or the affluent ones would foot the bill. With whisky poker, the cards determined the " shout." We played poker for drinks. But no one was permitted to lose twice. It sounds simple and rather childish, but we liked what developed into a mess rite.

One afternoon, while we were having tea in the mess, there was a stentorian yell outside, and Cam burst into the marquee. " I've broken the b——," he roared.

" Hell ! " snapped the Flight Commander. " Another crash ? "

" No," replied Cam meekly. " I mean I've broken her. Landed her perfectly, a three-pointer. Can you beat that ? "

" Go out and land her again whilst you have her tame," orders the Flight Commander.

Out went Cam and *exeunt omnes*. The Recording Officer rang up Wing, and all were on the spot to enjoy the fun. Cam took off. He had " tamed " her all right, for his landing was perfect. His service flying training was over.

Cam was never a dashing pilot. But he was steady and dependable. You knew that if Cam was pilot in your escort machine, you never had to worry as to whether the Hun would spring a surprise attack

on you.   Or that if you were going into action, you
need have no qualms as to Cam's side of your machine.
In all things, we felt we knew, Cam would be there
when you needed him.

The peak of Cam's flying career was reached
when he was selected as co-pilot to Hadji in the
Handley-Page, to open the final offensive on our
front.

Cam died a horrid death.   Beriberi.   At 14th
Australian General Hospital, Port Said.   They
buried him there.   As I mentioned before, he was
trained to fly with Tommies of No. 22 Squadron.
What did those instructors think of Cam?   Personally, I didn't know.   But, after the Armistice,
they travelled 240 miles each way from Aboukir to
Port Said to put a wreath on his grave.   If it was
only a courtesy, those English johnnies had enough
graves of their own to visit.   But it was more than
a courtesy.   It was a pilgrimage.

Cam left the squadron in 1918.   Officially, he
never returned.   But he was in our mess every
morning at eleven until the end of the war.   We
who knew Cam would come in for whisky poker.
And we'd deal a hand to an empty chair—we dealt
it every morning until the squadron disbanded . . .
I hope Cam got his drinks.   He used to like them
so.

The wooden cross reads :—" Lieutenant C. C.
Cameron, 1st Squadron, A.F.C.   Died on Service,
November 18th, 1918."

CHAPTER VII

In 1910 two lads met in a tent, in the camp of the Corps of Australian Signallers, held during the visit of Lord Kitchener. They were both full of military enthusiasm and got on very well together. The effect of reading American he-man literature, and the fact that the lads wore slouch hats—which seemed to suggest sombreros and virile, " we'll-show-'em " manhood—caused each to call the other " pard." For one, the term grew into a general nickname ; he is still Pard. Every flying-man worth his salt on the Eastern Front, and since the war, every worth-while pilot in Australia and New Guinea can fill in the surname. Maybe you're not a flying-man, so I'll introduce Ernest Andrew Mustard. We knew and know him as " Pard."

When war broke out, Pard was one of the first to volunteer for service with the Signal Engineers. The enlistment records show No. 6 as Corporal E. A. Mustard. He was a telegraphist, a good mechanic, and he was keen. It was not long before he was posted to the 1st Signal Troop in charge of one of the wireless pack sets. He was an extraordinarily adaptable chap. Seemed to be able to put his hand to anything. One day it would be a motor cycle of the D.R.'s to be fixed ; next day, an aerial, or ground earth mats that had gone phut ; one day a horse needed shoeing and the farrier was missing. Pard had never shod a horse before, but he did the job.

Then, with a happy grin, he would say : " Next, please." He would tackle anything. Not in an aggressively boastful way, but with the idea of service. He had enlisted to serve. Until the real thing came along, he was going to do all he could, and in the doing and the learning, he grew continually better qualified for the next job. I knew. I was the other " pard." And we were in Egypt together.

The extraordinary thing about all this general utility business was that Pard was absolutely self-taught. He was adaptability personified.

When his unit reached Egypt, Pard's skill and versatility soon became known throughout the 1st A.L.H. Brigade. While stationed at Maadi, the mess tables in his unit seemed to be more often in use for engineering than feeding purposes. This was typical of Pard : when he left his work tent, it did not mean he had ceased work. No, sir. He'd tinker in his living-tent, and if that wasn't big enough, well, there was plenty of room in the men's mess. I'm sure that not a few visitors came to the mess not so much to have a drink as to inveigle Pard into doing a job of work. He liked it. I think the best term to describe him is the American one— " trouble-shooter."

On 1 April, 1915, Pard and his wireless detachment left Egypt for an unknown destination. There were ten Australians and eight packhorses. Corporal Mustard was in charge. Only after we, the remainder of the Signal Troop, had arrived at Anzac did we learn that Pard and his detachment had landed at Helles with the 29th Division. Strange. I've never been able to find out what an Australian detachment was doing with this crack British division.

On the Peninsula, the quantity and the quality of the Turkish fire gave Pard ample opportunity to display his skill in effecting repairs. Remember, this was in 1915, when W/T was of the spark variety and contained many gadgets that were acutely susceptible to shell shock. But, as his log-books tell, Pard's sets rendered yeoman service. And weren't we of the troop pleased to see the little blighter back with us ! That was in May, at Anzac. He shared my dug-out until he dug one of his own.

For one reason I was pleased to see him go— he had an outsize in kits. And those dug-outs were only built for sleeping-room and protection— especially protection. When we were moved to the left for the Suvla Bay stunt, most of us only had a haversack, and an extra water-bottle or two. But Pard's kit ! When he had stacked it outside his dug-out, in Monash Valley, it looked as if it would require a full-size camel-train to move it. God only knows where he had collected it from, but, on appearances, he had souvenired every shell-case that Jacko had fired. I can still see him sneaking out at night for " loot." Oh, yes, and he also " specia-lized " in copper driving bands. What the deuce was he going to do with all the stuff we did not know.

But there it was. And we had to move three and a half miles, and most of it heavy going. Pard insisted that he was going to take his swag. While we were in the midst of a discussion *fortissimo*, of his parentage, Pard smiled sweetly and walked off.

An hour later he returned from the direction of the beach, trundling a wheelbarrow. Probably the only barrow on Anzac ; it was like Pard, not only to locate it, but to put over the required amount of tale to secure the loan of it. Anyway, he had it, and when he had piled his gear aboard, the barrow sagged. Pard was wiry and strong, but he was only a little chap. Solo, he couldn't move the barrow, and so Bert Billings was " requisitioned." With a couple of ropes, he pulled from the front.

The route lay through trenches, saps, open country, sandy beaches, up hills and down, and along valleys. What was called No. 3 Outpost was the destination. Pard got there—that's a habit of his —and with his dunnage. I wonder if some lucky people, who got little copper knick-knacks from Pard, ever realized the sweat and grit that lay behind them.

Although that incident was, in its determination and grit, typical of Pard, there was nothing spectacular in his career on the Peninsula. Just steadiness, solidness, and absolute trustworthiness. It wasn't until the Sinai campaign in 1916 that Pard began to make his mark as an all-rounder. But he was still an inveterate tinkerer. I well remember an incident at Romani. Pard was on leave and there came a rather impatient inquiry from Captain Gower, the brigade vet., as to whether Mustard had completed repairs to his watch. I said I'd have a look ; I knew Pard kept his watch repairs in a pannier. That pannier seemed to contain all the watches of the British Army in all stages of *hara-kiri*. Which made me curious. After Pard's return I kept tab. All those watches were made serviceable. Many parts had to be made. He made them. His Signal cobbers used to say :

" Give Pard three inches of copper wire, a couple of terminals, and a pocket-knife, and he'll knock up a wireless set."

He was transferred to the Australian Flying Corps in 1917, and there for the first time he had full scope for his service ability. He started off as an observer, and what splendid qualifications he had ! Expert telegraphist, mechanic, good shot, a born map-reader, and all the backbone about the place.

Pard was a natural improver. I mean he was always improving things. For instance, when he was issued with his first batch of flying-kit, he looked over the leather coat, flying-helmet, goggles, and gloves, and decided they could be improved. The coat was too long. So he cut quite two feet off the bottom, achieving a motor cycling effect. That protective fur flap in front of his flying helmet was unnecessary. Off it came. The goggles had a fur strip about one inch wide round the edge. That was cut off. And the gloves were too cumbersome. Exit gauntlet extension. When he made his début on the tarmac he created a sensation. At 8000 feet he realized why some of the old hands had been smiling so knowingly. Pard nearly froze. That was one of the few rare occasions when his improving wasn't . . . er . . . improving.

In a few weeks Ross Smith selected Pard as his observer. In the East that was something of an accolade. Then began the finest pilot-observer combination on the Eastern Front. Pard had no trouble in qualifying for his " half-wing," the badge of the observer, known in the service as the " flying ———." No, I can't put it in print. But it was a bright effort.

Our squadron, being equipped with two-seaters, had nearly as many observers as pilots on the strength. Each realized the value of the other. And the odd pilot who had no time for an observer usually was to be found shooting down his Huns in the bar of either Shepheard's or the Continental, in Cairo. Still, the pilots had a general jibe, a laughing one, at the " obs." In the Bristols a factory inscription on the side of the observer's cockpit read :

" This machine must not be flown with less than 160 pounds in rear cockpit." So the observer was rudely dubbed " 160 pounds of baggage."

In every possible sphere, except action, there was some sort of rivalry between the pilot group and the observer group. Of course, the pilots were superior beings, but that did not prevent the inferiors from voicing their views as to allegedly faulty tactics in action. Finlay could always be depended on to point out to such and such a pilot that he would certainly have got his Hun if he had done this and that. And if " Fin " needed backing for his attempts to educate and improve the pilots, his fellow observers, Pard, Hudson Fysh, Kirk, Farquhar and Letch were always " on tap."

Particularly in sport was this group rivalry keen. The pilots were too good at cricket, but, although Headlam was No. 1 in the pilots' golf team, the " obs " were too good there—Wally Farquhar could beat any two pilots. The pilots were the stronger in tennis. It was fifty-fifty in hockey. But those hockey games at Mejdel were bloodthirsty affairs. Pard was not a good athlete—he never " made " any of the teams, at least, not until, on the day of a hockey " test " match, when the observers' team was a man short.

The survivors will never forget that game.

Very early the pilots' team discovered that Pard had no knowledge of the rules of the game, and that, with customary adaptability, he made rules of his own. They were very simple: swipe any one out of the way, if he got between you and the ball, and then, when the opposition was disposed of, shoot for goal. Actually, he shot goals from all angles. And none cheered him more than his opponents— from outside the playing area. They were not deficient in guts; but whangs from a hockey-stick were decidedly unpleasant things. In an air scrap, one had to take what the other chap was permitted to shoot at one ; on the hockey field a little, sandy-headed, laughing chap was given a wide berth. It was Pard, rather than the observers' team, who won the match.

Pard chuckled for days afterwards. For that

matter, he chuckled almost at all times.   It was a medicinal, contagious chuckle, but it degenerated into a shame-faced giggle when he was trying to learn tennis and golf.   I was mug enough to try to teach him.   Pard was hopeless.   At tennis, he never got any farther than the miss-hit and giggle stage.   As a golfer, he was a friend to the club-makers ; that chap could break more clubs in more ways than our joint pocket could contend with.

In short, sturdy, snappy, wiry Pard was a complete dud at sport.

While I'm on the subject of pilot v. observer rivalry, I must tell you of another subject of contention—vocal prowess.   The " obs " were clean-cut winners.   In both quality and quantity they could out-sing the pilots.   True, they had one advantage : they always sang in a lump—six to a table, while the pilots were scattered about the mess.   But they were too good.   The songs they sang—and we sang, for that matter—were pungently virile.   That was a matter of no consequence.   But forty to sixty husky Aussies could certainly make the welkin ring.

Most of our favourite ditties are unpublishable. But the following are samples : The first (I've forgotten the title) was sung to the tune of Chopin's " Marche Funèbre," and our words ran :

Where will we be in one hundred years from now ?
Pushing ! ! ! up the daisies,
Pushing ! ! ! up the daisies,
Pushing ! ! ! up the daisies . . .
Where will we be in one hundred years from now ?

OUR FRIEND THE ENEMY!

A group of opposition pilots whose photograph was dropped by Felmy on our aerodrome at Belah. Felmy, second from right in centre row. The white-capped central figure is Felmy's brother who commanded this squadron.

The glorious, poignant second movement was sung to words something like this :

There let me be beside the river ;
There will I rest for e'er and ever,
There will I be in one hundred years from now,
        One hundred years from now,
            Hundred years from now,
                Years from now,
                    From now,
                        Now.

And then there was another song, the sad, sad, story that has since been amplified by the versifiers of the R.A.A.F.:

The gallant young airman lay dying, and, as under
    the wreckage he lay,
With the ack emmas standing around him, these
    last parting words did he say:
" Take the cylinders out of my kidneys, the con-
    necting rods out of my brain;
From the small of my back take the crankshaft,
    and assemble the b——d again."

To return to Pard. It was not long after he had joined the squadron that Pard's reco. reports and photographs were eagerly awaited by Wing. He was the Compleat Observer, and this was soon recognized by the older hands, as well as the Heads. His reco. reports contained all he saw—nothing more, nothing less—and everything set forth in the plainest, simplest form. If Pard said that Tul Keram contained thirteen M.T. (motor transport)

K

and fourteen B.T. and S. (bell tents and shelters) they were there. If he reported that he fired sixty rounds at a Hun, he fired 'em. If his Combat Report mentioned " H.A. (hostile aircraft) shot down out of control," it was waste of time to check up. That Hun *was* shot down.

In many ways we were a jealous lot. When a small body of men—our normal officer strength was 50—live so closely together as we did in the service squadrons in Palestine, and with so few distractions; when luck plays so big a part in life all the time, when So-and-so gets assigned a job that promises fame and promotion while you have a lousy routine task that must be done ; and when there is so much time in which to brood—well, one's sense of proportion, of justice, gets weakened, and jealousy gets a toe-hold and digs in.

And yet, here was Pard, a mere tyro, attracting pats on the head from the Big People, while not a few old hands, who had always done their best, and a good best at that, were still in the rut. But there never was any jealousy so far as Pard, or the Ross Smith-Mustard combination was concerned. Both were outstandingly, superlatively good. Rather than jealous, we were proud of them. After all, it was *something* to have the finest two-seater team on the Front.

In fact, we were quite sure that they were the finest pair in the world. True, the cracks on the Western Front might have had much bigger " bags." But then they had so many more machines to take toll of. Taking into consideration the very big difference in numbers and scope, we were sure that the work of our champions would more than bear comparison with the best in the west.

To return to our winged mutton: Pard's first decoration was unique. It was an Order of the Nile. Only one or two of them came the way of the A.I.F. General Chauvel got one. But after the handshake, or the pat on the shoulder, with which we others congratulated Pard on his first decoration, there arose a storm of ribaldry. The noble order came in for all kinds of abusive comment. Finally a name was coined that met with general approval: the Nile boil. Rather foul, perhaps, but not unappropriate to describe its fiery centre and generally swollen appearance. Later on, Pard was awarded a Distinguished Flying Cross. More kudos, more congratulations. Wing took him over on two occasions as Staff Captain. Pard, however, did not take kindly to staff work ; so, in due course, his rusty head was to be seen once again sticking up above the cockpit of 1229.

Now, don't get the idea that Pard went his way about the aerodrome, his helmet bathed in halo light, everywhere smiling happy faces to greet him. On the contrary Pard and his tent mate, Alister Kirk, were heartily execrated for their excessive zeal with regard to machine-gun ammunition. They intruded their work and their views. They littered the mess with their " doings." They were missionaries. They were nuisances.

Of course everyone, pilot or observer, who valued his hide, used to pay attention to ammunition. But he and Kirk were fanatics. They nearly drove the armourers mad. They were always testing, experimenting.

By the way, there certainly was scope for experimenting with the ammunition. There were eight kinds : common or ball ; armour piercing ; tracer, and another variety of the same type, Buckingham ; Pomeroy and Brock, both explosive ; incendiary and Sheriton. We were allowed to make our own choice in the composition of our belts and drums and pilots usually differed from observers.

Here were two favourites with pilots : 2 rounds common, then 2 rounds armour piercing, then 2 rounds of tracer, then 2 rounds of Buckingham. This composition would be referred to as 2-2-2-2, mix. " Mix " means " and then the same again and again." Like a repeating decimal. The other was 3 common, 2 tracer, 1 armour piercing, 3 Buckingham, 2 incendiary, 1 Sheriton. This would be designated 3-2-1-3-2-1, mix.

Observers had their own tastes and would use their own judgment in the composition of the drums of the Lewis guns. For ordinary purposes, the following were popular : 2 common, 2 tracer, 2 Buckingham, 2 armour piercing, 2 Pomeroy (2-2-2-2-2, mix) ; and 2 tracer, 3 common, 3 Buckingham, 2 armour piercing (2-3-3-2, mix). For ground strafing, 4 common, 2 tracer (4-2, mix) was the customary selection. Most of us were able to standardize.

Not so Pard and Alister. Always, they were striving for a better drum. That was all right. But these fanatics set out to know every bit of the gun

by its Christian name ; to learn the innermost
secrets of every why and wherefore. I think Kirk
was partly responsible—he had been a commander of
a machine-gun section before he joined the squadron.
He was a specialist. But Pard, although not un-
familiar with machine-guns, had most experience of
them opposite the business end of those used by the
enemy. Anyhow, he soon caught the disease too ;
but the armourers had stronger terms than that for
the intense interest he and his pals displayed.

It was not long before bolts, ejectors, return
springs, gas chambers, and firing-pin had no secrets
from Pard. Then you would find him arguing
with Alister as to whether the return spring should
have umpteen pounds as per the instruction book,
or—

"Come along and we'll try it out on the range.
Sergeant, give us another drum of common—
Thanks."

Out they would go. We would hear the shooting at the range ; and we would hear the arguing
when they returned. It was a subject that never
could be settled. Still, it must be admitted that the
pair had fewer stoppages than any one else in the
squadron.

They were a happy pair, but there were occasions
when they saw red. I forgot to mention that not
only did they show excessive care in the composition
of their machine-gun drums, but they also had the
drums specially protected by cheese-cloth and other
wrappings. That was when the drums were
awaiting use. Each drum after it had been fitted,

with every bullet hand picked and polished, would be carefully wrapped up to keep out sand and dust. But not everyone in the squadron was as careful and zealous. When the need was immediate, and the sluggards had no drums of their own ready, Pard or Alister was the loser.

Pard had one other sore point—his moustache. Or rather what he intended, hoped to be a moustache. After years of striving it remained a negligible collection of anaemic sandy hairs.

As with Ross Smith, Pard made his mark as a war-bird, and then flew to a wider fame as a civilian. First, however, he carried on in uniform when the Royal Australian Air Force was established. Quiet, unspectacular work this. This highlight in Pard's career was his aerial survey of the Great Barrier Reef, the first ever made. When he resigned the service, he was more or less one of the flying mob. Then he went to New Guinea and flying had its début there.

Edie Creek had proved to be a phenomenally rich goldfield. But it badly needed suitable transport. The field was 7500 feet above sea-level and separated from the coast and civilization by densely wooded mountains. Only a distance of forty-six miles, by air, but it took a white man eight to ten days to cover the 100 miles land-route, and the native carriers could only do five or six miles a day. There was gold in " them thar hills." Fortunes of it. But a road was out of the question. The cost would have been vastly, disproportionately expensive. What then ?

Along came little Mr. Mustard. There was another man with vision up there. Also, this other man had money—Guinea gold.

On 18 April, 1927, Pard Mustard flew from Lae (on the coast) to Wau, near the goldfield. It was the pioneer flight. His D.H. 37 carried a payload of 600 pounds, which represented the work of fifteen carriers for three weeks. The flight took an hour and a half. Thereafter, New Guinea had wings.

Pard was the moving spirit. He pioneered, established, and managed the air transport of Guinea Airways and Bulolo Guinea Gold. By 1934 the service had carried 19,364 tons of freight and 12,000 passengers. Its associate company, Placer Development, carried to the fields four 1250-ton dredges— in pieces of course. But probably you know the details ; they are aviation history.

Two particular feathers in Pard's helmet must be mentioned : one is, that the service he started and managed until this year is universally regarded as outstandingly the finest air-freight " show " in the world ; it has averaged 20 per cent. dividends for seven years. The other is, that one of these planes —a W34 Junkers—has done eleven trips in one day, carrying 19,500 pounds of cargo inwards, as well as back loading. Pard spent six of the last eight years in New Guinea.

Now having had enough of the tropics, he is back in his native Melbourne. He looks the same sandy little runt. His moustache is still a failure. But his name is now Mustar. Anyway, what is a *d* or so to a chap like that ?

CHAPTER VIII

KINGS OF MEN

IF ever I have enough money, I am going to Germany. I want to meet two Germans. I know one of them by reputation, and by his machine-gun-belt arrangement. By the way, I hope he is not still using it. He is now, I understand, a pilot with Luft Hansa. He used to be a lieutenant in the East. The other chap was a captain. I have forgotten his name. But I shook his hand when he was on his way to a prison-pen—a prisoner. What I think of the pair is indicated by the title of this chapter.

During my second trip over the line, I had my first action. I was the observer in a B.E.2.e flown by Jack Potts. Upon many a previous occasion I had had the " wind up "; that time it was blowing a full gale. There were two reasons: Archie and Felmy. In those days of our slow and clumsy 2.e's and 2.c's, the German gunners on the ground had excellent targets, and the No. 1's, whether pulling gun lanyards or pressing triggers, were excellent marksmen. With Archie filling the heavens with little balls of black wool, their concussions making the old bus stagger and tremble, I could feel plenty of moisture upon my forehead and around my neck.

And when white ribbons began to zip about the machine and I managed to identify them as tracer bullets, I was frankly scared stiff.

On the ground, one becomes accustomed to lethal things being hurled about, but in one's first aerial action the machine seems to take on a new fragility; the ground is so far away; and I had seen crashes in the raw. My eyes were fixed upon the ground, for I had to " read " it—I was doing a reco. Imagine what would happen, I was thinking, if Archie scored a direct hit ! Or if one of those tracer bullets set fire to our machine, killed the engine, or cut away the controls ! But my unpleasant speculations, instead, were soon cut away.

" You —— fool," roared Potts, " get that gun going before it's hanging up in a Hun mess."

Instantly I became conscious of the split-second present. It was easy to get the gun in action, but exasperatingly difficult to bring fire on the chap whose tracer bullets were flying around. He, I learned later, was none other than Felmy, the Hun cock-of-the-walk on our front. Potts knew it, and was zigzagging with all the cunning of which he was capable. At last I got Felmy in the sights and gave him a burst—and, by the way, no Lewis gun ever threw a bigger cone. Then, as opportunity offered, four or five more bursts, until Felmy broke off the fight and went home.

Why he went we could never understand. I would love to think it was because of my splendid shooting. But it was not splendid shooting ; my hands were too unsteady. And poor old Potts never kidded himself that he could fly better than Felmy. We did not pursue Herr Felmy.

However, we were not out of trouble. Whoof ! . . . . whoof, whoof . . . whoof ! Archie, with no wish to hit the wrong machine, had ceased fire while Felmy had a go at us, but was again permitting its joy to be unconfined. Our engine, an R.A.F., was hit. It developed St. Vitus's dance ; shook and shuddered, and seemed bent upon throwing itself off its bearers. Potts promptly put the nose down and, with engine full on, streaked for our line. Thanks to the height we had when Archie got us, we were able to reach home.

The noises the engine made kept us from feeling lonely, but we had thoughts, goose-fleshy ones, for company. No wonder the engine was noisy. Archie had wiped out one of our eight cylinders. Part of the con-rod remained, but the piston must have gone with the cylinder. Bad enough to happen to a car engine, but up in the air. . . .

In the mess that night I felt a bit better. They were telling stories about this Felmy ; how, after he had shot down Palmer and Floyer he had flown to our aerodrome, and had dropped letters and photos telling the news, and photos of them amidst their captors. There were stories of other German pilots, too, who, it seemed, also had their chivalrous points; when the chance offered, they showed up as sports-men. With an air of " welcome to our happy home, and depart in peace," they allowed our chaps to fly over the Hun aerodromes, and drop kit for those of our lads who had been taken prisoner, and all that kind of thing. So I reasoned those Huns could not have been such terrible people.

To return to Felmy. He was obviously Public Enemy No. 1 on our front. " A crackerjack pilot, and a splendid shot," declared our Flight Commander, and that Albatros he flew was nearly twice as fast as our 2.e's, and as manœuvrable as they made 'em. In our innermost thoughts we new chums hoped he would have an early death—a very early death. He did not. Only a few days later he was on the job again. . . . Vautin, one of our " loots," got tangled up in a scrap and lost to Felmy, making a forced landing in the enemy's territory. He was posted missing until Felmy dropped in with the tidings. Vautin was a prisoner. Promptly, Murray Jones flew to the German aerodrome mentioned and dropped Vautin's kit and letters.

At this stage I must explain a pleasant war-time courtesy which existed between the gladiators of the air. Usually a prisoner taken by either side was sent back to a prison camp as soon as possible. But when a squadron took a prisoner—shot or forced down—they would keep him at their show for days. The prisoner had the freedom of the mess, and once he gave his *parole*, he was almost a free man. If wounded, every care and attention were forthcoming.

To revert to the *affaire* Vautin. Early one morning the squadron was aroused by a Hun alarm— the klaxon horns brayed fiercely, and the gongs clanged :

" Hun machine approaching, flying low." So ran the report. A single machine did not act that way unless it had an olive-branch in its mouth.   In a matter of seconds we realized this German pilot was on a peaceful mission.   This notwithstanding, we watched the machine very closely—to study its manœuvrability.   We might meet that particular plane in the air some day, and then the knowledge would come in mighty handy.   Well, this bus came in very fast—that is, judged by 2.e speed.   The pilot waved, flew a circuit round the aerodrome, tossed a message-bag on to the tarmac, looped, almost as if he were putting thumb to nose, and sped away. The message bag brought tidings of Vautin—in a letter that was surely one of the brightest missives of the war.   This is it:

ALL DEAR SPORTS,

My joy was very tall to receive your many letters.   To-morrow Vautin comes, to take *all* the things and *all* the letters (with photo) which were dropped.   He is such well educated and genteel boy, that we do with pleasure all, what is pleasant for him.   But if you write for us, you must write more distinctly, because our English is not so perfectly that we can read all ; the most legible writings has firstly your writing-machines, and secondly Murray Jones.   Vautin has me talked very much of him.   I hope to fight with this sport more oftener.   I thank him for his kind letter—I thank also for the decoration of the " Rising Sun " from Mr. Lex Macnaughton. Perhaps I can see the sun later in Australia. Too my very best thanks for the photo of Mr.

Brown and for the kind letter and many photos of R. F. Ballieu.

For order to answer your questions : 2nd Lt. Steele is unfortunately dead. He expired 20.4.1, soon after his imprisonment. He was shot down by our archies. (2) Mstr. Heathcote is in captivity and well, I think in the same place as Mstr. Palmer and Floyer.

Murray Jones is a very courageous man, we have feeled it in flying and when he came to drop the things for Vautin so down (perhaps 100 feet) I would like to have his address in Australia, to visit him and a photo of him and the others, but— I beg—a little more bigger the photos, because I could scarcely perceive your sport-eyesights! " Ramadan " is not practical for a visit at you; one must fast all the day. For souvenir I have exchanged my watch with Vautin, and we have engraved our names. Where can I disperse more an aqueduct ? Hoping, our good condition is continuing long time. With best wishes for all, who have written to us ! With sportly respects,

Your G. FELMY, Oblt.

I beg, this letter not to send in a newspaper.

Please send the photo with X to the parents of Mr. Vautin.

Just in case Felmy's English is a bit too broken, and the references pass you, perhaps a few words of explanation will be in order. The " writing machines " were, of course, typewriters; and Murray Jones's writing was far too good to be true— he'd never make a doctor. The decoration of " Rising Sun " is a neat one—Felmy was referring to the standard A.I.F. badge. I wonder if he was grinning when he called it a " decoration." It is not difficult to translate " eyesights " as meaning eyes. But there's more than meets the eye in that question, " where can I disperse more an aqueduct ?" Even if you substitute " blow up " for disperse. You see Felmy had scored a bull's eye on the aqueduct at Mustabig and his query was a gentle gibe. But we did not answer the question. There was quite enough scope for enemy bombing without us serving up a target on a silver salver, as it were. And the first of his postscripts, the tail before the horse one, does not need any explanation to those who have experienced the War Censor. Reproduction of letters from the front was not done. Imagine how Felmy would have fared if his letter had been published and the German authorities had learned of this fraternization.

As it deserves to be, that letter is in the Australian War Museum.

It is very difficult to say where this mutual chivalry actually commenced, but as far as our front is concerned, the first record of the enemy's participation in this sort of thing relates to what took place in May 1917.

Our squadron was then quartered at El-Arish. A bombing formation was on its way to deal with Junction Station, when a Hun, flying at about 2500 feet, appeared over the drome. The spectators on the ground expected bombs, but the German pilot (Felmy, it proved later) only threw a message-bag and made off homewards. Before his mission was correctly interpreted, two Aussie machines took off after him, but failed to catch him. The message-bag contained two letters, from Palmer and Floyer (captured officers from No. 14 Squadron), and a letter addressed to a German prisoner in our hands.

No 14 Squadron immediately sent two machines to the German aerodrome at Beersheba with a reply to their note, a " thank you," and an apology on behalf of the Aussies for sending up two machines against their messenger.

Potts " got his "—Potts who had introduced me to Felmy and Company. He crashed on the enemy side of the line, and they buried him with full military honours. Felmy's letter told us of the affair. Felmy's photo showed us the grave, and Felmy's machine brought the tidings. But this time he did not loop before he flew away from our aerodrome. There was a gentleman for you. We drank toasts to Felmy in our mess.

The year 1918 was busy for war-birds in the East. Our casualties increased—shot or forced down over the lines. But in all cases the utmost consideration and courtesy was extended by the German officers to their prisoners. We did all we could to reciprocate. That " the other chaps " were appreciative, is indicated by the following letter we received in German :

To
    THE ROYAL FLYING CORPS,
        Palestine.

The German airmen thank you for the chivalrous treatment of the crew, Lieut. Haugg—Lieut. Hauck, and we beg you to convey the clothes that we drop down.

        A GERMAN FLYING SECTION.

And there was this letter received by Haugg when he was a prisoner-guest at our squadron:

        O.U. 6.11.18.

DEAR HAUGG,

    The warmest wishes from me and all men, that your life is saved.   We are very grieved to hear of poor Lulla's death.   Can you kindly ask the Royal Flying Corps to drop in our lines the photo of Lulla's grave in order that we may send it to his parents?   Your distinguished work in landing the aeroplane shall never be forgotten, even in the service.   We hope that the clothes we have dropped for you, will reach you safely, if the parachute is not damaged in the air.

    A most friendly regard to the gentlemen of the Royal Flying Corps ; and you, friend Haugg, from the depth of my heart, I wish you early convalescence and a joyful greeting after the war.

        Yours,

        F. R. WALZ.

This type of fraternizing with the under-dog was not limited to squadrons in the line. Flying officers

LIEUTENANTS PALMER (IN SKULL CAP) AND FLOYER (GLENGARRY)
In German hands, with the wreckage of their engine. Responsible : Captain Felmy,
second from left.

used to visit the prison camps ; have a word with His Majesty's war guests, and, more important still, leaves smokes, sweets, and etceteras. That the Huns did not do so much in the way of prison visiting was due, I'm sure, to the fact that they did not have so much spare time or the scope for gifts. G.H.Q. did not regard this fraternization with favour, but, although we were " tipped off " to that effect, no actual official instruction, so far as I know, was ever issued forbidding these manifestations of mutual regard.

I have left until last the best example I know of chivalry in air warfare. From June 1918 onwards, things were hectic along our front. Allenby was throwing full weight into every punch he had, and Jacko smothering up and back-moving desperately, was trying to avoid a knock out. But nothing could save him, and he went down for the full count on 31 October.

In the meantime, we flying chaps had to earn our pay. Every day there were bomb raids, combats, recos, and special missions. When Allenby's general advance opened on the morning of 19 September our activities were intensified. That very day consternation was apparent on the other side of the line. The enemy's communication had been destroyed; his railway junctions disorganized (we bow modestly); our cavalry were ripping through the break effected by the artillery and infantry on the enemy's right flank; and the German airmen were ground-bound at their aerodromes. But Archie was as energetic as of yore. He had more targets than ever, and he

L

fought a gallant last round, considerably increasing our casualties.

Archie was on the job when we put over our biggest single bombing attack, on Afule, then the enemy's main railway junction. Twenty-five machines participated. Considered in the light of later-day mimic air manœuvres over London, Paris, and Rome, twenty-five machines does not sound very many. But it was an outstanding show for us in 1918.

And, in case you are sniffily superior, I will have you know that this quarter of a hundred machines did lay their eggs as per instructions. Machine after machine rained its bombs on the targets.

Archie succeeded in putting one engine out of commission. A direct hit. The pilot tried to glide home, but did not get that far. He was forced to land near Jenin, almost cheek by jowl with the largest German aerodrome on the front. Quite a good landing—machine, pilot, and observer all in one piece. But a most unhealthy locale! However, the crew of a Bristol Fighter of No. 1 Squadron, A.F.C., which was out on patrol, had seen the Tommy machine go down, and they followed to see how things fared with the gentlemen in the *consommé*. When some 6000 feet above the stricken machine, the Australian observer suggested to his pilot that they " give it a fly."

" What ! Land and pick 'em up ? "

" Why not ? If they could land O.K., so can we. It looks good enough to get down on."

" Righto. You watch the sky and I'll concentrate on the landing. Here goes ! "

The distressed machine had landed on a level piece, but, as the Aussies' machine swept down, the crew saw a disquieting sight on the German aerodrome—there were five machines on the tarmac and three of them had their engines running. Nor was that the only cause for apprehension—as the Australian came in to land, the pilot discovered that a deep wady in front of him would not permit him to alight. Engine on, he made a circuit and then put her down on the other side of the wady. The Tommy pair left their machine—apparently so pleased at the prospect of rescue that they forgot the rather important detail of destroying the plane by fire, as laid down by instructions—and ran towards their rescuers.

As the former were negotiating the wady, hundreds of natives seemed to appear from nowhere. They ran towards the English pair, and judging by the way they were brandishing their weapons, were emphatically hostile. The natives had come from a nearby village—overlooked by the rescue machine. Thus late, the rescue crew remembered that there was a price of £40 on the head of every British pilot. Jacko paid—in gold—when the natives delivered the goods.

The Australian observer was quick to take in the situation and yelled to his pilot:

" Turn her to starboard so I can bring my guns to bear on them. . . . That'll do. If they come any closer I'll fire a burst or two over their heads. You watch out for our passengers."

But the natives, Bedouins they were, could see

two, and possibly four, £40s awaiting their dirty
fingers. They cracked on the pace, firing their old
blunderbusses as they ran. No time, now, for
foolin'. This was war. The observer aimed his
double Lewis not over the Bedouins' heads, but
down amidships. Rat-a-tat-tat-tat. It was impossible to miss. Gaps appeared in the Bedouins'
ranks and down they went, wounded and
unwounded, to take cover.

" Here they come," roared the pilot.

" What, more of 'em ? "

" No, our passengers and get an eyeful of the
size of 'em. He must be fourteen stone if he's a
pound. . . . Can't be helped. Toss everything
we won't want overboard—spare ammo. camera,
photo plates, rations, every blasted thing. An' get
out of your flying-togs. We haven't a dog's
chance of getting off unless we're as light as an
omelette. I'll watch the ' Beds ' in front."

" Righto," says the observer. " Everything's
out. I've only got two drums and they're on the
guns."

" Pitch 'em overboard ! If we meet a Hun we'll
be easy money in any case—those drums can't save
us. . . . Hey you (to the British observer) sit on the
floor of the back cockpit, with your back against the
front bulkhead. Understand ? And make it
snappy."

" Right," said the Tommy, and promptly disposed himself.

" And you "—to the Tommy pilot—" you'll have
to sit on the Scarff gun mounting. Face the front,

FELMY'S HEART-WARMING LETTER

put one leg on each side of me, and hang on to the centre section struts. Up you get ! That's O.K." And there rescuee No. 2 sat, on top of the fuselage between pilot and observer, with his legs in the " office," one on either side of the pilot. " Now, hang on ! An' if we crash taking off, remember the Beds—they're in the crop just in front."

The Bristol with her double human load, moved slowly forward under full throttle. The 375-h.p. Rolls-Royce seemed to realize its responsibility. The pilot swears that it produced two hundred more revs than ever before. The machine rolled, staggered, and lurched over the rough ground—but it was gaining speed all the time. Up came the tail, and the pace increased, up to flying speed. She was off ! Cheers from all concerned. But suddenly came an unpleasant thought—what of the Huns ? The excitement of getting off had excluded the memory of that nearby Hun aerodrome, complete with five planes on the tarmac, and three of them with the engines running. Yes, those machines were still on the tarmac, with the officers and men around them, but not one of them attempted to take off.

Why ? That question persisted as the Australian machine began another most hazardous manœuvre. Immediately ahead was a mountain range, 3000 feet high; the machine had to get better height than that, and there was only one way and one place to get it—slap bang over the Hun aerodrome. So right there, before an intensely interested German audience (the Bristol quartet could see them only too well), the machine circled, with slow turns, and, seemingly in a million years, attained sufficient height to leave for more pleasant surroundings.

It arrived home, and, after a five-minute intermission, during which the quartet mopped their brows and had their backs thumped by the lads . . . but you are not invited to join them in the mess.

After all, that was only an incident, and the offensive went on, the advance being general. Two days later, the Light Horse pushed through Jenin, and came upon an aerodrome, capturing quite a number of German officers and men. That a land unit should capture flying men—on " terra-cotta " of course—is an indication of how rapidly Allenby's attack was being pushed home. There was not time for the usual Flying Corps courtesies to enemy prisoners wearing wings. So the Jenin crowd percolated back through the pens to Richon, where British General H.Q. was situated. Five of these German Flying Corps prisoners, ex-Jenin, were on their way to G.H.Q. for interrogation when an Australian pilot came up. He asked the guards' permission to have a word with the Huns, and, this having been granted, the party sat down beside an E.P. tent. " Have a Gold Flake ? " asked the Aussie as he proffered his case. " Thank you, sir," replied the five in turn, in good English. That made it easier. " Well, it's this way," explained the Aussie ; " this is an informal matter. I see you are members of 301 and 302 Jagdstaffel from Jenni."

No reply.

" As you can see, I'm a member of the Australian Squadron, and I wish to satisfy my curiosity upon a certain matter. The war is nearly over, so what about it ? It is only a personal matter."

The German party consisted of a captain, and four lieutenants. They looked at each other, as if seeking a decision. Then:

" Yes, we belong to Jenin," replied one of the lieutenants.

" Good. Were you there on the morning of 19 September ? "

" Yes."

" Did you see a British machine effect a forced landing alongside your aerodrome ? "

" Yes. We were all watching it. It was a D.H. 9 from the English No 142 Squadron."

" Right. And did you see another British machine come down a little later and rescue the crew of the D.H.9 ? "

" Yes. That machine was a Bristol Fighter and belonged to your Australian Squadron." This from another lieutenant.

" Quite right. Now this is the point of my questions: You had five scouts ready on your tarmac, with pilots standing near by, and I suppose you had machine-gunners at their posts on aerodrome guard. But not a machine took off, not a shot was fired at the Australian machine, and it was a long time over your aerodrome. Why ? "

The German captain jumped to his feet, saluted and clicked his heels in the best German style, and spoke for the first time:

" Sir," he said curtly, " sportsmanship is not confined to the English! "

As I said before, if ever I have enough money, I am going to Germany to try to meet two Germans —Felmy and that captain.

CHAPTER IX

" CHARLIE "

WHEN it first showed up at the squadron, we laughed uproariously. Then we asked two questions : " What the hell was its breed ? " and " Where did it come from ? " You'd have laughed too, if you were seeing " Charlie " for the first time. He was a dog. A dog with the nose, head and tail of a Pomeranian; a dachshund's body, plus the turned-inside-out legs of the breed ; bulbous Pekinese-type eyes; and an expression that said : " What if I am a mong ? Me, I'm built for use." He had too, a beautiful soft brown coat, with a white bib on the chest, and a fuselage of about the size of a Peke. Even if we had had an X-ray at the squadron—which we hadn't—we wouldn't have given Charlie the " once-over." If we had, we would have dis-covered that Charlie had an outsize in brains and hearts. We were to learn of these in more con-ventional ways.

Charlie made his squadron début one morning at the aerodrome at Weli Sheikh Nuran. He just turned up. In those days, dogs were as unpopular on aerodromes as they are now. As we learned to our cost, whirring propellers seem to bring out all a dog's curiosity and pugnacity. And it's too late to train a dog after he has snapped at a moving prop. There were other reasons why dogs were not popular.

But this funny little intruder was so different. After we had fruitlessly and pungently discussed its breed we inquired as to ownership. We learned that an officer of a neighbouring squadron had brought it to our parts, after a spot of leave in Cairo. We took him over, and gave him a name. Charlie was a wonderful dog.

Mascots were no novelty to us chaps in the East. Our squadron had gone through a wide range, from kangaroos to the imported goat. Which latter, if I may say so, was a loathsome animal. One had eaten my favourite shirt, and for good measure, as it were, had then sicked on my stretcher. But we took to Charlie without reservation. Even Mick accepted him. (You remember Mick—he made his bow in Cam's chapter.) Charlie made an immediate hit when he was taken on strength. He settled down to squadron life, and soldiered on under the leadership of Mick. Julis, Mejdel, and then, at Ramleh, Charlie was promoted to O.C. mascots—by succession. Mick had aged, and, after contracting the last of several virulent doggie ailments, he suffered so that death was a relief. He died a soldier's death—with a bullet in his brain.

When Charlie took his place, he was accorded a very high honour—I became his custodian. And Hadji, my tent mate, was permitted to share his company . . . and his fleas.

Charlie soon threw his weight about. His first objectives were the dogs from the nearby villages and jackals from the hills. These were continually on the prowl around and through the aerodrome.

Furtive ravenous brutes they were, especially the big scraggy jackals, whose favourite food, judging by our personal losses, was tooth paste, boot polish and soap. But Charlie, a veritable David amongst these Goliaths, never shirked a fight. At least he'd dash fiercely at the intruders, to which he was about knee high, and judging by the tone of his barks, he was using Digger-like language.

Invariably the dogs and jackals bolted. They would return, however, for the aerodrome was too big a place for one little runt of a dog to patrol ; besides Charlie liked his "shut-eye." So the jackals returned, and, notwithstanding Charlie's sallies and our precautions, there was much canine thieving.

We decided to lend Charlie a hand. Six Mills bombs were borrowed from the armourers; and some "high" meat from the cooks. The pins of the Mills were removed, and the handles held down to safety. Then, that night, bombs and meat were taken out to the centre of the aerodrome, and linked up by lacing cord. The idea was for the jackals to take a piece of meat, and by moving it, to tug at the cord, and thus release the handle of the bomb. There were six reports during the night. When we went out to investigate next morning, there was jackal strewn all over the aerodrome. Unmilitary but effective.

Charlie was also a most valuable factor in our campaign against even more unpleasant intruders— snakes. They were green brutes about two feet long, and according to the natives, very venomous.

I never heard of any of our forces being bitten.   But, on appearances, that was no fault of the snakes. They lived in the crops adjoining the aerodrome— corn, barley, and a kind of millet called dura.   But when the terrific heat of summer split the aerodrome surface, the snakes went a-visiting.   They'd lurk in cracks in the ground, and, although they could be seen, they were hard to get at.   For the cracks were often 8 feet deep and only a few inches wide.

The snakes increased so greatly in numbers that official measures were taken.   Organized daily searches were made.   Once the snake was located, the drill was to pour about a gallon of old petrol into the cracks on both sides of the reptile, and then ignite the petrol.   The snake would be driven to the surface and the troops would declare war with cudgels.

Charlie was immensely interested in this war. He appointed himself a private scout, and many a time his frenzied barking attracted the snake-hunters to a quarry.   If the clubs did not finish the job, Charlie had the sense of anticipation, and the leap of a Test slip fieldsman; and a set of teeth.

We got to love this quaint plucky little cuss, but we could not blind ourselves to the fact that he was a thief.   He took every opportunity to improve his rations.   Apparently he did not regard bully-beef as an improvement.

On this subject of rations, we, of the Flying Corps, were slightly favoured.   We were, so it was said, the Suicide Club.   You know: roosters to-day, and feather dusters to-morrow.   Anyway, the average

AS HONOURED BY GENTLEMEN

The grave of Lieutenant J. Potts at Jenin. He was shot down by Germans ; by them buried with full military honours ; the remains of his propeller were set at the head of his grave ; and the grave was reverently tended.

casualty hours over the line were something like five or six. . . . After that it was the hospital or sad slow music. Which may have influenced the A.S. Corps to try to make our short life a better fed one. So, if there was any fresh meat or bread on the sky-line we used to get first " chop." Perhaps our proximity to the ration distributing centre may have been the reason. Still, we got it. The meat ration was frozen beef or mutton—which, when it reached our cooks, was so hard that to cut it up, axes were used. Charlie was like Longfellow's school kiddies who used to stand outside the village smithy and watch the sparks fly. Only he was watching for flying chips of meat. As mentioned before, Charlie was a splendid slip field. He knew that unless he took the catch clean, he, poor doggie, would have a Mother Hubbardesque fate. Besides, I'm sure the little chap was a sportsman at heart—it wasn't so much the meat as the sport of fielding it that drew him.

Still, it must be confessed that Charlie was a glut-tonous meat-eater. There was that afternoon for instance, when Hadji and I were having a snooze, and a grunting and snuffling outside the tent made us investigate. There was His Lordship with a whole side of mutton. He had souvenired it from the cook-house, dragged it through the lines, and was apparently just about to plant it in our tent, when we took a hand.

Why hadn't Charlie started his feast ? Because the mutton was frozen. Frozen so hard that the thief's teeth had left no mark. We were not a little

embarrassed when, with the body in the bag, we
went down to the cook-house.   Renwick, the chief
" babbler," was a sport.   And he liked Charlie.

" No one will be the wiser," he said after looking
at the side of mutton.   We all enjoyed the roast
that evening.   But only two of us knew of its cruise
across the desert.

Most well-trained dogs will spring off their hind
legs for a worth-while prize.   Charlie used to go one
better than that.   Come with me down to the squadron range, and see for yourself.   Oh yes, every
squadron had its range, and since we all of us knew
what happened to bad shots or slow ones, we spent as
much time as possible in target practice.   Not only
with Vickers and Lewis guns, but with revolvers and
shot guns.   Why shot guns, you ask ?   Well, they
were on issue, and with clay pigeons (also on issue)
they were excellent training for snappy work with
eye and trigger.

Well, here we are, and here's Charlie.   Watch
him—he'll go straight along to that Lewis.   Now
bring out your Jack Gregorys!   Ever seen better
slip fielding ?   The little blighter is trying to catch
the shells as they are ejected.   And you'll remember
they pump out at up to 460 shots a minute.   There,
he's caught one!   See him shake his head ?   That's
not a gesture of triumph.   That's pain.   The
shells are piping hot.   Here, try one yourself. . . .
Believe me now ?   But there's Charlie on the job
again.   The thrill of pulling off a catch seems to
console him for any discomfiture.   The little fire-
eater seems to love the noise and the bitter smell of

cordite. And please note that Charlie never makes the mistake so common to us superior beings—he keeps clear of the business end of the guns. We never taught him that. Innate wisdom.

Charlie was no " Tarmac Admiral." He had his flying, and over the line, too. His first flight was with Ted Kenny and myself. Ted had the front seat; I was the observer. We thought it was only going to be a quiet patrol at 16,000 feet. And we made another initial blunder: while pilot and observer were suitably clad to withstand the cold, the third member of the crew was only wearing his usual clothes. So when I saw him huddled up on the floor of the cockpit, and obviously chilled, I picked up the little cuss, and put him inside the front of my Sidcot suit. There he was quite comfortable, thank you, and every now and then he poked his head out and surveyed the upper world with obvious approval.

Then I forgot Charlie—a Hun had got stuck into us. When my twin Lewis began to bark, Charlie also went into action. No, rather he retreated. Every time I fired a burst, Charlie wriggled down farther, and by the time the combat was broken off, he was right down my left leg. And there he had to stay until we landed.

But Charlie had guts. He made no demur when next he was offered a flight. And he liked the new possie we had for him. When Archie was whizzing about, or the guns were talking, we'd drop him into the fuselage. There he'd dash up and down, and although the roar of the engine prevented us from hearing him, we could see that he was barking furiously.

Nor did Charlie's air sense stop at that. He knew his bosses' machine—1229 Hadji's and 4626 mine. Always he would go down to the tarmac with us and watch our machines take off. Soon he got to know them. The moment either 4626 or 1229 put her wheels down, Charlie would rush out to the aerodrome and bark his " welcome home." Hadji and I would always stopy taxying and haul him into the machine. Of course, we were proud of Charlie's little performance, and soon the squadron knew about it.

Many's the time the mechanics tried to trick him. They'd point to a machine just about to land and tell Charlie things. But the little blighter wouldn't budge. He was waiting for us, and us only. On occasions eight machines landed at one time, but Charlie never made a mistake—he identified ours, and ours only he went out to welcome with his barking.

For all this manifestation of esteem Charlie was not given many trips over the line. You see there was a war on, and although it was great fun having a little dog in a plane, that kind of thing could not be overdone. All told, I think Charlie did not have more than six flights. But he managed to improvise another kind of squadron transport. Every flight had its zog, a kind of two-wheeled jinker, with aeroplane wheels. The zog was used to facilitate the movements of planes on the ground. It had a shallow box in the centre of the axle, which accepted

FELMY AND ANOTHER "BAG."—LIEUTENANT C. VAUTIN OF OUR SQUADRON

the tail skid of the plane; and a long handle by
which the plane was hauled about. The zog was
also used to carry ammunition, camera gear, etc.

Well, Charlie " adopted " the zog of " C "
Flight—the flight to which Hadji and I belonged.
At every opportunity he used it as a carriage. If it
was trundled out to the tarmac in use, Charlie would
trot along as an escort. But the second it was
empty Charlie would spring into the box. Nothing
strange about this procedure, except that the little
dog would use only " C " Flight's zog. It wasn't
that the mechanics of the other flights were not
willing—on the contrary they strove to entice
Charlie on to their zogs. But the dear little cuss
was a one-zog dog.

Charlie's best turn was impromptu. It happened
at a squadron concert one night. We had a really
good concert party, one of the leading lights of which
was Joe Gilberg. He had a nice baritone voice, was
a capable pianist, and had a gift for parody—the
pungent kind so popular with the troops. Joe's
speciality was a parody dealing with doings at all the
reconnaissance areas.

Now, just before the concert in question, the news
leaked out that Charlie had a " sweetie " at a nearby
native village. Something had to be done about
this. Something vocal, I mean. Oscar Bennett,
another leading spirit of the party, collaborated with
Joe Gilberg, and they produced a song about
Charlie's amours. It was screamingly funny, but
rather too biological for reproduction here. Well, at
the concert, the composers were just in the middle of

M

their song, when Charlie pattered on to the stage.
It was quite unexpected, and when the intruder
cocked that funny little head of his on one side and
looked down at the audience, the whole hangar
howled with laughter. Whereupon Charlie retired
in good order.

But the songsters never completed their song.
Hardened performers as they were their own
laughter was too much for them. To this day there
are members of that audience who will not believe
that Charlie's entrance was not rehearsed. They
are wrong—only Charlie was responsible.

While the troops on the Western Front specialized in chats, our verminous speciality in the East
was fleas. That is clumsily put, but you know
what I mean. Not a few of us in the squadron had
graduated from chats to fleas—we had suffered the
former in front-line soldiering on the Peninsula and
elsewhere. But although fleas were not so bad as
their smaller colleagues, they were still bad enough.
In fact, during Charlie's reign they were such a
plague that Keating's was the second best seller in
the mess canteen. (Yes, you're right—beer was No.
1.) The fleas used to hunt in packs, and unless you
sprinkled your sheets and pyjamas every night,
there were unpleasantly busy times ahead of you.
Despite our barrages of Keating's, Charlie's fleas
multiplied to such an extent, and at such a rate, that
something had to be done about it.

As usual, Hadji had an idea—a petrol bath.
That sounded right, so Charlie was dumped in an
inch of petrol in an enamel bath, and Hadji and I

proceeded with a flea purge. We could see the immediate casualties, but after about half a minute, when we were just warming up to our work, Charlie howled with pain, jumped clear, and sprinted away. Only then did we realize that the petrol had burnt Charlie. We set off to repair the damage, but the little dog was in terror-stricken agony, and it was only after about a dozen of us had rounded him up were we able to catch him, and remove the cause of his pain. A drastic, a too drastic treatment it had been, but it proved effective. Charlie had no further trouble with fleas, at least for a time.

Of course, when the whole show was over, and we had handed over the box and dice to the Tommies who took over our squadron, we took Charlie with us. An old pal like that had simply to go back to Australia with us. So down to Kantara went Charlie and when we marched down to board the *Port Sydney* for home, he was with us. But only that far. The chief officer said no ! Because of the regulations. He would not listen to reason. He could not be bribed. He was too vigilant to be eluded. So, after hours of unsuccessful wrangling, we had to face the cruel fact that Charlie was to leave us. A snap decision, and Charlie was handed over to an old admirer, an officer in an R.A.F. squadron. That was a hard wrench. Charlie had become as much a part of the squadron as the very planes. But at least we had one consolation—he was in good hands. Of course we arranged to get news of him. And the laddie who gave the promise kept his word. Charlie stayed on with his new boss until the latter

was transferred to a squadron in England.   Then
he went to Paris, " on the staff " of the Air Attaché.
He died there in 1922. . . . Charlie must look
darn funny with wings, and the canine equivalent
of a harp.

CHAPTER X

AGENT X

I HAVE heard of Madame X; the algebraic X in
my youth harrowed my educational soul; and I have
had, at one time or another, some little experience
of our old newspaper friend X-marks-the-spot.
But of all the X family, the member I best know is
Agent X. A good friend of ours in 1917 and thereafter. As is too often the case with friends, Agent
X had its faults ; but, all in all, Agent X was very
popular. Almost it shared with *La Vie Parisienne*
the honour of being first favourite in the squadron
mess.

First a word about *La Vie*. Few of us in the
East had a working knowledge of French. Even
fewer of us had been to *La Vie's* home city. Still,
for all our linguistic failings and lack of travel, we
could and did appreciate French humour, in word and
picture. In the East there was hardly what could
be called a happy medium in written or pictorial
humour. The Gyppos specialized in dirt, and the
English newspapers or magazine humour was not
quite salty enough for most of us. A joke or a funny
picture that in these piping days of peace may set
you chuckling would have fallen flatter than a spilt
egg over there. War, somehow, blunts lots of finer
feelings, toughens one's sensibilities, and calls for
more condiment in one's entertainment fare. Just

169

one instance of this and then we must go on to hunt up Agent X. In the early days, lots of the lads had personal pictures in their huts, or in the cockpits of their planes. Round about 1917 and on, *La Vie Parisienne* supplied most of the pictorial ornaments.

Now about this Agent X. In 1916 Von Sanders, the German Commander-in-Chief of the Turks, established a big wireless telegraphy station at Damascus, then hundreds of miles behind the line. Any one with half an ear knew it had Telefunken equipment—Telefunken sets had a peculiar note all their own. Well, this station used to issue orders to all and sundry of the enemy forces. It moved divisions, brigades, battalions; it ordered new gun positions; it directed the German aircraft to do this, that, and the other thing. For instance, in the last-mentioned sphere, when machines were ordered to reconnoitre a certain part of the British front, the time, height, route, and report centres would all be specified—all dot-dashed out over the air for friend and foe to hear.

Of course it was in code. Therein Fritz made a very bad bull. He thought the code was British-proof. It wasn't. Late in 1916, or early in 1917, our Intelligence discovered the key to the code, and thereafter, with special listening stations established to record every signal sent out from Damascus, we had an ear cocked at the keyhole of the enemy Higher Command. We called the Damascus wireless telegraph station Agent X.

No need to tell you how valuable this information was. Especially to the Flying Corps, for in those

days we had poor machines, compared with the
Albatros Scouts, A.E.G., Aviatik, and D.F.W. two-
seaters of the enemy.   Agent X apprised us of all
kinds of interesting stunts about to be undertaken
by the opposition.   So, as soon as you received your
orders for the next day, you would wander along to
the Recording Officer's den to learn what Agent
X had to say about the movements of the German
machines on the morrow.

It was a comforting thought to find that your
times and area did not clash with the movements of
an Albatros or two.   On the other hand, if you
were fortunate enough to be flying, say, a B.E.12.a,
and you were warned for an H.A. (Hostile Aircraft) patrol, your first move would be to consult
Agent X, who, with Intelligence as an interpreter,
would apprise you where the best hunting was to be
secured.

There was one gem of news that Agent X whis-
pered into the pearl-like ear of Intelligence.   It
mentioned a new railway, running from Lezzun towards Kara.   That *was* news.   Next morning our
machines verified the report.   They brought back
photographs to prove it.   Whereupon the bombers
went out and did their stuff.   After two or three
raids it was too hectic for the Turks—they went on
strike.   That railway was never completed.   Agent
X got another good-conduct stripe.

But there were times when Agent X misled us.
Deliberately or otherwise, I cannot say.   Come
along to the tarmac and hear some of the conversation
on this subject.

" Why so glum, Les ? "—this to Lieutenant Les
Spragg, him of the perpetual smile.

" Glum ?   So'd you be if you had relied on Agent
X as I did.   Every (dot-dash) time I cross the line
lately, Agent (dash-dash) X informs the world that
the Hun will be somewhere else.   And then the next
thing I know is that I'm a (dot-dash) Aunt Sally for
the German Flying Corps.   Blast it, if I have to
dive 6826 (a B.E.2.e) much more in the way I have
had to, to get away from the Huns, I'll pull those
(dash-dot) extensions off."

" Rot ! " from one of the mob.   " You always
would winge."

" Winge be (dash-dot-dotted).   I hope some of
you coves strike Agent X in a bad mood.   To my
way of thinking he's no agent of ours."

" To hell with that " (" Little Matt " speaking).
" You've been trying to co-operate with Agent X
and didn't know it.   Anyway, what's wrong with a
Hun or two ? "

" You can have the Huns and Agent X, too."
snorts Spragg.   " All I want is an hour to climb to
my height (8000 feet); another hour to do the job;
and fifteen to twenty minutes to get home.   And
finally I'd prefer clear pure air undefiled by the presence of any foreign intruder.   That's my idea of
fighting this war out of a 2.e."

" You don't want much, do you ? " asks another
friendly tormentor.   " But you'd better have a
drink and forget it."

And while I'm on dialogue we can let Agent X
churn out some more dots and dashes (not the

parenthetical type above !) while I tell you of another conversation that had us laughing for months afterwards. It started with a question by a curious pilot. Or maybe I should say by a pilot who was curious:

" Charlie," he said, " how long did it take you to get your height over the rendezvous to-day ? "

" Well," said Charlie (Lieutenant C. Watt), " we climbed and climbed and climbed. You see, our escort from No. 14 Squadron was to pick us up at 8000 feet over Belah. We could see them up above all right, but after climbing for an hour, the 2.e observer and myself had reached the majestic height of 6500 feet."

" Well, what did you do then ?   Go over ? "

" Of course. You know what sort of a reception we got from Archie of Sharia and Irgeig. And to make matters worse, on the way back we must have a brush with a Hun two-seater."

" Filled in your combat report ? " interjects the curious one.

" Combat report be damned; as the engagement was fought at 600 yards' range, there was no need for that. The Hun wouldn't and we couldn't close the range. So there we were ! "

Then he added reflectively: " What a pity our thoughtful War Office doesn't equip our guns with telescopic-sights. Anyway, *Comic Cuts* next week will report that the dashing British pilots still maintain air supremacy on the Eastern Front ! "

Comic Cuts, I had better explain, was our name for the R.F.C. *communiqué.*

Then there was the time Agent X brought us news that some German machines were to land and report at Juj at a specified time. British scout machines like the Bristol Bullet and D.H.2 would be present at the right time, but the results were usually indecisive. The speed and manœuvrability of the Hun machines offset the element of surprise. In those days, with our old tubs, it was most difficult to shoot down the enemy planes.

"Ding" Turner, and "Useless" (Eustace) Headlam, the squadron's two crack artillery observers in early 1917, could tell of several instances when Agent X was a liar. Huns would appear at the wrong time or in the wrong place. Whereupon the observers, in their old crates, would have to cancel in a hurry their talks with the artillery.

Then there was the time Agent X's news indicated that a certain sector was to be unvisited. So one of our two-seaters went there to do an artillery shoot.

Everything started well. The battery had been accurately ranged. "Fire for effect" had been wireless-telegraphed, and the pilot and the observer had settled themselves in a dress-circle seat to see a Turkish dump blown to hell, when rat-tat-a-tat and a string of tracers reminded them that there was a war on. In those days the observer was responsible for the supervision of an artillery shoot. But as our battery commenced to throw "four-fives" on the target, the observer had more pressing matters to attend to than the war on the ground—three Aviatik two-seaters were diving on them. So, while the

" ob." returned the fire, the pilot hurriedly up-
anchored and left for home.

For some reason or other, the Huns did not press
the engagement. Our plane got away, but very
much the worse for wear. Whether the Huns had
mis-read the map co-ordinates, or our operator
had been mistaken, or Agent X was putting over a
" double-cross " we never learned. But when
" Mark Antony," the wireless officer, wanted to
know how the shoot had turned out, Eilwhart, the
" ob.," told him. There are some punches which
even a simple recounter of plain, hard facts has to
pull, so you will have to imagine just how the pilot
expressed his views. I heard them. Marvellous !
He was just cooling down when Mark asked if any
Huns were seen.

" Huns! Man, at one stage the sky was full of
'em ! And the only (hush! hush!) thing they didn't
hit was that dud Sterling set you wireless blokes
think is the last thing in radio."

Mark was conciliatory :

" Oh well, better luck next time."

" Better luck be ——," howled Eilwhart, now
red about the neck. " It's a pity you Sparks blokes
haven't got to do your share over the line. Here am
I after being shot up the rudder, and providing
three Huns with a miniature Roman holiday, and
you have the —— gall to say ' Better luck next
time! ' Mark, you an' your shoots can go to hell!
Give me recos or photography. This —— business of flying round and round and round the one
spot for hours, an' Archied like hell, an' just

waiting for the Hun to pick you up, is up the pole."

"But," says Mark, "Agent X said nothing last night about Huns appearing over Sharia."

"Agent X," retorts the observer, "is just as reliable as your Sterling sets. Ask 'Bones' what he thinks of both Agent X and Mr. ——Sterling."

"I know Bones has no time for Agent X," agrees Mark.

"For him? I should think he hadn't. He swears Agent X made a date for him and Muir with a dashing Albatros over Beersheba. They shot their way out of that date, but since then Bones prefers not to listen to Agent X. He is concentrating on *La Vie*."

As I said before, sometimes we did not know whether Agent X was misleading us. On one occasion the evidence was very much against him. One of our 2.e's, returning from Beersheba, spotted a Hun down near Khalasa. This was reported to the squadron. That night Agent X referred to the loss of a two-seater in that neighbourhood. Early next morning six of our machines set out to bomb it. Arrived over the target, the observers, aided by the early morning sunlight, immediately discovered the plot. The plane was a dummy. Where was the trap? Pilots opened their throttles and released their bombs and climbed all out. Yes, there were Huns—two of them. Albatroses. They were diving from the sun. It was an inconclusive action. A few rounds were fired, and the speedier Huns got away. The name of Agent X was mud.

All things considered, Agent X was a very handy

chap in the early days. As the Royal Air Force (Vice-Royal Flying Corps, deceased 1918) expanded and we got more modern machines, there was not the same need for his warnings: we could look after ourselves. Agent X remained in action until late in the piece; but by 1918 you never heard him mentioned, except reminiscently.

But he proved one very important thing—that our Intelligence had done a fine job of work.

CHAPTER XI

THIS chapter tells the story which, up to the present, has been concealed behind a brief and cold official *communiqué*, and a bombing and machine-gunning report. The former told only the final fact ; the latter, a tissue of white lies, cloaks one of the most audacious " stunts " of the Eastern Front.

The official *communiqué* ran : " A German two-seater was destroyed by machine-gun fire." What really happened was this :

On 28 September, 1918, our G.H.Q. ordered a special reconnaissance of Damascus. G.H.Q. was very curious. It wanted to know whether the Turks were trying to bring down fresh divisions to hold up Allenby's general advance. G.H.Q. wanted to know as much as possible—about troops, camps, trains, roads, and so on. Damascus had not previously been reconnoitred. It was then many miles behind the lines. A long trip, and the Bristol that went out on the job carried extra petrol in tins; the observer refilled the tanks as the occasion arose.

For a week very little had been heard of the Hun. He had received a terrific gruelling. Most of his aerodromes had been captured. If he had any machines left they should be at Damascus; we knew he had an aerodrome there. Still, that was a minor detail—the main thing was his ground doings.

The Bristol flew over Damascus at an altitude of 6000 feet, to be greeted by a few Archies. Then to " count " the worth-while things below. To the novice, everything appears to be all jumbled up. Only with continual practice can correct estimates be made of what is down below, and the various positions plotted.

Damascus was a hive of industry that morning. Trains choked the station and the sidings; there was a great deal of motor transport on the roads; two large camps held troops. After careful observation and analysis, it was ascertained that most of the movement was from the south to the north—away from Allenby. This was very heartening. Jacko was not making any special efforts to stem our advance.

The big job done, the pilot remembered the Hun aerodrome. There it was—seven hangars, and a machine on the tarmac. But no movement. No time to find out why. A last look round before turning for home. Then, the pilot received a thump on the left shoulder—that was the observer's signal that there was a " Hun on your port " (left). Picture the succeeding moments! Engine goes on full, up comes the nose of the " Bif " in a climb. Where is he ? The observer points to a dot, thousands of feet above.

" What's he doing up there ? " muses the pilot. " Hasn't seen us, anyway. I'll see if we can sneak up to him. If the sun was higher I could climb out of it, to him. Well, here goes for under his tail."

Up climbs the Bristol, towards the Hun, who is

flying round Damascus in a big circle. The Hun is unaware of the approach, but the Bristol pilot is taking no risks—it may be a trap. Now the Bristol pilot can see that the enemy is a two-seater, either a D.F.W. or a Rumpler. And at a distance of 1000 feet an unusual deficiency is noticeable—no rear gun. Either the gunner had it inside the cockpit, or he had forgotten it. Whatever the cause, that makes things much easier for us. Up climbs the Bristol. No sign that the Hun knows of the approach. Until the noise of the Rolls-Royce engine over that of the Mercedes causes a long fair face to pop suddenly over the edge of the German gunner's cockpit. When it saw the British markings of the Bristol, back it popped. And stayed there.

The German pilot was still blissfully unaware of the proximity of the Bristol. A burst from the forward Vickers soon apprised him. He looked amazed, dumbfounded. But the Bristol was then on his starboard side, level with him, and only 40 feet away. He could not use his front gun—and he had none at the rear. The observer of the Bristol had him covered with his twin Lewis guns. He was " cold " ! But he couldn't be shot down in cold blood. What then ? The Hun was now flying north—away from the lines ! Away from the Bristol's home. That was no good. The " Bif " pilot taps the Hun on the shoulder, so to speak—by firing a shot. Then he points south and waves the Hun around. The latter does as he is told; goes round in a gentle turn. The Bristol pilot holds his original position about 50 feet away and slightly to the rear. Thus placed, he begins to shepherd the Hun towards the British lines.

This goes on, mile after mile, and it looks as if the first capture in the air is about to be effected. No further move from the German gunner—he is still out of sight in the cockpit. Quite likely he has fainted.

When the lines are showing under the leading edge of the machine, the Hun starts a slow turn to the left. Round comes the Bristol like a sheep-dog edging an erring sheep back into the fold, and cuts off the turn. Then the pilot points towards the British lines, and pats his gun. He is saying in a language that the Hun understands—" Do as you're told, or I'll open fire." The Hun understands. But, as captured and captive come over the lines, the Hun pilot is obviously getting fidgety. Suddenly he acts. With throttle wide open, he goes down in a power dive, but the Bristol pilot has not been caught napping. He dives, catches the Hun in his sights. . . .

You have read the *communiqué*.

Quite a lot of things had been done by our squadron that were not exactly according to Hoyle. For instance, an enemy officer had been captured behind his lines by a plane crew, and flown back a prisoner. Attempts had previously been made to bring back Hun crews as prisoners, but, owing to bad take-off surfaces, the ambitious captors had had to be content with the Huns' flying-kits as souvenirs. Nunan had his " sledge " and Tonkin his " batteries." We used to hunt gazelles by air ; the observer, armed with a service rifle, made the kill. We used

N

to " borrow " Avros to go fossil-hunting. And there was good reason for the order—promulgated in 1917—which said :

" Pilots must refrain from using their aircraft to further their matrimonial prospects."

But the venture which is about to be told was surely the most exciting, madcap affair that ever was put into effect on the Eastern Front. The story, surely, would have been told many years ago but for the fact that all concerned were bound to secrecy. That bond has since been lifted. But, even now, I am not mentioning names. Believe this, though: I know all the facts, and they are only facts that I am giving you.

The two pilots concerned, X and Y, had worked out the scheme months before. It sounded good to them, but they could not put it into effect without the co-operation of the Recording Officer. He was absolutely against it—he did not wish to lose two good friends, or the squadron to lose two good pilots, and probably a good Bristol. But X and Y importuned, and the R.O., being quite sure that the opportunity they sought would never occur, eventually agreed to help, and to secrecy. Then the two conspirators went about their preparations. Secretly they secured some bombs, and discussed the plan from every angle.

The impossible happened. The opportunity arrived when an observer came in with a report that a German squadron new to our front had arrived, and was in the process of establishing itself. Promptly X, the senior of the two conspirators, came to the R.O. and requested permission to go out and take photos of a new anti-aircraft battery position.

" Rot," snapped the R.O. " We don't want photos of those things. We want 'em bombed."

" Splendid," says X. " Am I to understand that you will fix it with the C.O. ? "

" Yes," replies the now thoroughly miserable R.O. " But understand you're to bomb that Archie and nothing else."

" You don't doubt my word ? " retorts X, looking hurt. " I promise you there won't be enough of that battery left to make a paper-weight, when I've finished with it."

" Righto. Good luck."

" Just in case the battery shoots us down, will you post these letters for us ? " (They were to their next of kin.)

" Certainly, old man. But I wish to God you weren't going. Oh, you lunatics. But . . . good hunting ! "

A little later a Bristol is run up and, a fact that caused no little comment on the tarmac, the rear cockpit contained not an observer, but a pilot, and he had some queer gear. I shall let you into the secret. The objective was the new Hun aerodrome. The queer gear was made up of incendiary and Mills bombs. The intention: to land on the aerodrome, and play merry hell with the hangars and aircraft. Previously, and afterwards, that job was always done from the air. X and Y had the idea that it could be done more thoroughly from the ground. Let the R.O. continue with the tale:

Three hours after she left, old 1229 returned. She looked all right. The two madcaps came to me grinning.

" Got those letters I gave to you before we went out, old lad ? "

" Of course I have. Thank God I didn't have to post 'em. But what I want to know is how you got on."

" Sshh ! Not so loud. But, believe it or not, we didn't find that Archie battery."

" Really," says I, all sarcastic. " Did you try very hard ? "

" Of course we did. But we remembered one or two of those standing instructions about bombing Jacko and shooting up nasty people. So we just carried out those orders and here we are."

" Righto. Come into the office and fill in the bombing and machine-gunning reports. Then, perhaps, you will be charitable enough to tell me just what did happen."

" We'll tell you later to-night, when we can be alone. But not before."

I had to be satisfied with this. But I guessed, from the grins on their dials, that their jaunt had not been without success. And when the blighters invited me to come to the mess and join in the toast of " confounding our enemies," I was certain they had done the Hun no good.

The spots did not loosen their tongues! They were tantalizing swine. There was nothing else to do but wait. Dinner dragged on and on. And, when they left the table, they told me that they had decided to play a rubber or two of bridge. That meant that they'd play until " lights out " and then there would be a scurry to reach one's tent before the electrician finally threw the switch.

But they relented slightly. After they had played a rubber, they winked at me and then sleepily said good night to their bridge opponents. When, a little later, I reached my tent, both were sprawled on my cot. X tells the story :

" Well, old lad, we did it. But now that we've put in a bombing and shooting-up report, not a word to a soul. Promise ? " Promise given. " Well, when you saw us off, we didn't exactly expect to get back by old 1229. We thought we had a good chance of pulling it off. But we carried a wad of Turkish sovereigns and piastres; they would have come in handy if we had had to entertain our Turkish captors. Still, you know—just in case, we left the letters to be posted. Nothing exciting in the trip over the line. Bit of Archie. We didn't give ourselves away by flying straight to the new aerodrome. Made a detour and came on in from the rear. That report was right. Two single-machine hangars were up, two more were being erected, and one was laid out on the ground. Three two-seaters were handy to the hangar sites, and through the open doors of the two erected hangars we could see two more. Couldn't see any aerodrome machine-gun guards.

" We came down fairly low and dropped the Coopers, one by one, hoping to send the mechanics to cover. That was a win. They immediately sprinted towards an adjacent village where a few trenches had been dug. Then there was a trifle of 'vertical gust.' We couldn't find their wind indicator, so we had to chance the wind being from the same quarter as when we took off here. We got down O.K. but it was a funny feeling putting your wheels on a hostile aerdorome. Everything seems different—different noises, different smells, different machines and hangars and layout. Everything was strange, including the rate of beat of my heart."

" Me, too," chimes in Y. " I wasn't feeling too happy."

" Well, I taxied her fast towards the hangars and turned her round so that we could get off in a hurry if we were attacked. There wasn't a soul to be seen. So Y goes into action. Gosh! He looked a scream as he lumbered away from the machine. He had three incendiary bombs under each arm, a Very pistol stuck out from one of the pockets of his Sidcot and the butt of his Colt from the other. As soon as he got away I ducked into the rear cockpit to cover him with the Lewis. You should have seen the poor cow trying to sprint towards the first two-seater. . . . You did look a sight, me lad. Anyway, he hadn't forgotten his drill when he got there.

" First, he fires a shot from his Colt into the petrol tank. Then he gives her one from the Very to ignite the petrol Up she goes! It was a D.F.W. and it burned like a bonfire. The next machine wasn't so obliging. The Verys wouldn't get her going, so Y hauls off and lets drive with an incendiary. Up she goes ! Two tries, two victories.

" Then, while Y was running off towards his next target, I took a tumble to myself. I'd forgotten all about my job in watching his. You see, I had the Bristol ticking over at about 400 revs. Couldn't cut it down any more in case she choked. You know how the engine behaves if you keep it idling for any lengthy period. Anyway, I gave some attention to the machine and then I sat up with a jerk—a machine-gun was rattling away. I couldn't locate it, but I opened up with both Lewises and sprayed the farthest edge of the aerodrome. That quietened 'em. Then I looked round for Y. He was running away from a machine . . .

" Yes, I know. You shut up—I'm telling the story. You went after the machine out in the open, and slightly back towards the Bristol. Then our friend, the German gunner, opened up again. This time I located the cow, but I couldn't fire on him—the wings were in the way. So I had to turn the Bristol. Then I hopped back into the rear cockpit, and gave him the remainder of both drums. I whipped on two fresh drums, and gave him another burst or two. He didn't open up again.

" When I turned to see how Y was getting on, he had his third bonfire going and he was walking towards the last machine. All of a sudden, about twenty or thirty men with rifles ran towards the aerodrome. This wasn't so good. So I roared to Y to get aboard. But the silly cow was too interested in making his final bonfire. He was ' poop-ing ' off the Colt and the Very in succession, but he couldn't set fire to that bus. So I jumped into the front cockpit, intending to taxi down to him and . . ."

" Just a moment! Just a moment." This from Y. " Now *I'll* tell you what happened. When I heard the engine, I thought this old hound was going off without me. No, it's no use your looking all hurt an' sad; I did think you were going to push off without me. So, after heaving my incendiary and Mills into the Hun machine, I went flat out for the Bristol. It was moving away from me, and the Hun riflemen had opened fire. I could see that our machine was gaining speed, and Gawd only knows how I did it, but I managed to get alongside and grab the Scarff mounting with one hand. Then up comes the tail—you'll pay for that one day, me lad—and there I am streamlined down the top of the fuselage. You, you may laugh, but if ever I had the wind well and truly up, it was then. Anyway, eventually the gentleman at the controls condescended to allow me to get into my cockpit.

" Then we flew round and checked up the result of our attack on the "—he grins at the R.O.—" er, anti-aircraft battery. Three D.F.W.'s were burnt to the ground, another was slightly the worse for fire, and one hangar was blazing fiercely. Which I may say, with due humility, was not a bad effort. And our only cost is a few holes in old 1229's wings."

This is the true story. The following day an official bomb raid was launched against the new squadron. Observers reported that before the

bombs were dropped, the Germans had had a fire—
one of the hangars was burned. After that raid the
squadron was, to all intents and purposes, wiped
out.

I have been mysterious in the writing of this
story, because there really was a bond of secrecy
involved. But I was released in 1920. Since then
X has folded up his wings for keeps. Already I
have written a chapter about him, and I do not think
dear old Hadji would mind me telling this story now.

Some Australians were born unpopular, some
achieved unpopularity, and others had unpopularity
thrust upon them. The Aussies in Alexandria in
1918 could not quite make out the whys and the
wherefores of the matter, but the fact remains that
they were most unpopular with the headquarters of
3rd Echelon. Maybe a certain degree of blindness
was in evidence when Tommy officers appeared within saluting range. And perhaps the Aussie's off-
parade manners were not based on the book of
etiquette. We had some tough 'uns in the " Ack
I Fuf." But the majority of the lads were not better
or worse than they should have been when off duty.
Anyway, the fact was brought home to the Aussies
that they were not the white-haired laddies at
H.Q.

The news reached the Aussie " Huns " at the
flying training school, Aboukir, and a deep dark
scheme was hatched. It concerned the C.O. of
Echelon and the Sporting Club at Sidi Gaba, which
was midway between Alexandria and Aboukir.

The Sporting Club was a *de luxe* affair—polo-ground, golf-links, tennis-courts, and a racecourse with flat and hurdle tracks. Luxury plus. The links extended across the inside of the race track. Well, one of the Aussie " Huns " who was floundering through his early solos discovered that at the same time each morning a staff car left Alexandria and came to Sidi Gaba. Arrived at the club-house, the car would always disgorge a short, fat chap, who, accompanied by a caddie, would later come out to the first tee at the same time every day.

One morning the Aussie flew down to have a look-see. Yes, there could be no mistake—it was the C.O. Echelon. The pilot had met him in person, and in circumstances that had caused the C.O.'s face, figure, voice, and manner to remain a vivid and unpleasant memory. So as the pilot flew back home he did some thinking. A brain-child was born. It was greeted with howls of joy in the mess.

Next morning broke cameo-clear, and by 7 ack emma three small dots appeared high over Sidi Gaba. At its usual time a staff car pulled up at the club-house, and three figures alighted—three shadows to the pilots high above. One was a tall unknown. One, short and skinny, was the caddy. And the fat tubby shadow. Oho! The pilots look towards each other and nod happily. Simultaneously the throttles are opened, and the noses of the planes are pushed earthwards. The descent becomes a screaming dive as the short fat shadow sets about addressing the ball. More speed as the club goes up and back, and then, as the club-head begins its journey towards the ball, three Nieuports thunder into the picture. The three shadows move and crouch as the planes, engines full mouthed and wires screaming, supply the " follow through " and then zoom away.

One plane breaks formation and takes to the hurdle track. It races along and takes the hurdles with verve and *élan*. The other planes follow suit. When the aerial steeplechasers are on the far side of the course, the fat shadow begins to move again on the first tee. Again the planes roar into the golfing picture, flat out, but this time low. Just above the ground. The fat shadow moves again. There's an uplifted club in one hand and it is pointing angrily aloft.

Robert Bruce's spider had nothing on that fat shadow. That is so far as persistence was concerned. After each aerial visit it would move violently and then settle down to a familiar stance. Whereupon the " Nieups " would again intrude. Finally the fat shadow loosed a golfing Archie— clubs, bags, and balls were hurled aloft. And as three shadows moved away from the first tee, back to the club-house, the pilots again looked to each other and smiled happily. Almost they could imagine the words . . .

The second act to the comedy started when the staff car left the club-house. Then the three Deadly Sins swooped down and gambolled and frolicked above the car until it reached the outskirts of Alexandria. Finish comedy.

Followed a tragedy. That very evening there appeared on the notice board in the officers' mess of the flying training school at Aboukir, the following :

> In future no machine on early morning flying will fly within a radius of two miles of Sidi Gaba Sporting Club. Instructors will be responsible for the carrying out of all flying training within the close proximity of the aerodrome during this period. Any breach of these instructions by pupils must be immediately reported by instructors.

A. A. ANDERTON, Lt. Adjutant.

I don't know whether the despot's golf improved. I hope not.

CHAPTER XII

" FELUCCARING "

WEBSTER defines " felucca " as " a small, swift-sailing vessel, propelled by oars and lateen sails—once common in the Mediterranean."

The word is a noun. There is no verb. That is, there was none until 1916, when the troops in Cairo coined the word. It was used only in the present participle—" feluccaring," and I doubt if the word will ever be accepted into the dictionary. But it had a vogue ; and it now brings back interesting memories. I like to think of the word as having what could be called three " moods," to wit : feluccaring proper, feluccaring improper, and feluccaring *de luxe.*

First of all, about " feluccaring improper." You would get leave and go to Cairo. A charming lady would honour you with her company. Let us imagine that it is one of those wonderful Egyptian nights—oriental sights, oriental sounds, a glamourous moon, and, strange but true, a heartening wad of piastres in your pocket-book. Less than half an hour's drive away is the Nile—the very sound of the name is romantic. Yes, the lady would like to go on the river.

Now this brings us to the felucca. In fact, there are lots of feluccas. They play a big part in Egyptian transport—as most of it is done by water.

They are stodgy, clumsy craft, not unlike English canal barges in size and hull, but their rig is quite different. A felucca has two masts, and two sails, the latter rather like isosceles triangles set at a jaunty angle. There is a certain something about the craft that seems to blend with palm-lined shores, white villas, colourful, smellful boatmen, and moonlight—especially moonlight—on leave . . on the Nile.

We are not interested in the ordinary feluccas—the cargo-carriers and so forth. It must be something befitting the occasion. The Arabs know it:

"Felucca, mister?" they call. And persuasively, "Me give you General Blank's for 10 piastres."

We make a selection—there is plenty of scope. Some of the craft are really luxurious affairs, prepared for wealthy tourist traffic. They have ottomans, divans, excellent Oriental tapestries, incense. It is all very Eastern.

We make our choice. Our *wallad* poles out a few hundred yards into the stream. If the *wallad* is an old hand, experienced in the ways of Aussies, the passengers soon hear two splashes, a few seconds apart. The first is caused by the anchor, the second by the wallad diving overboard, *en route* for the shore. If the *wallad* is new, or badly coached, something has to be done about it. The colour of his teeth, the shape of his nails, the cut of his clothes—there's something wrong about the fellow. Somehow he clashes. He's a blot on a romantic riverscape. Hence ! Powerfully you place your boot where it

will do most good, and overboard goes the felucca
man. Then he swims ashore. He knows you
won't steal the felucca, and that you'll need him
again.

When you do want him, he is easily summoned.
There's a gong in a conspicuous position on the felucca. You strike it. If your ear is sensitive, you'll
hear a faint splash from the shore, and not so long
afterwards a moist, grinning *wallad* clambers
aboard. No hard feelings. He philosophically
hoists the anchor, wields his pole. *Et voilà.* . . .
But I never could remember the Gyppo for " Home,
James ! " That, at all events, was feluccaring
improper.

Feluccaring proper was wholly and solely a flying
job of work. Luckily for the Egyptian transport
system, it had a very brief vogue. As follows:
Among those undergoing flying training at No. 24
Squadron at Aboukir, Egypt, in 1918, were some
Australians and South Africans. They got on ex-
cellently together, and when the Afrikanders were
transferred to a fighting training squadron elsewhere, their colonial colleagues gave them a bumper
send-off. The final stage of the beano was the
" shooting up " of the train—the train that was
carrying the South Africans away to Cairo. " Shooting up " as done in the approved Flying Corps
style.

The Australians, in single-seaters, did all the
stunts that they knew, and some that they had never
heard of, above the moving train, whose roof was
swooped on from all angles, to the great delectation

of the " guests," and the consternation of some of the passengers. About sixteen miles out of Alexandria the aerial farewell concluded.

In these parts there are many large canals on which feluccas are used extensively; and it was unfortunate for the gentlemen in command of these vessels, that a number of mischievous war-birds were in the vicinity upon that bright summer morning.

Turning away from the train for home, Pard Mustard, the leader of the formation, flew just over the top of one of these craft. He was climbing steeply with full engine on, with the other planes following suit ; the pilot of the last machine in the line happened to look down in time to see a felucca on its side, and sinking. Back on the squadron tarmac, this member of the party mentioned the incident to one of the others. No, said the latter, he had not seen a felucca sinking, but he had seen one with a dangerous list; probably it had struck bottom. That started a discussion.

Pard listened, said nothing, and suddenly dashed back to his machine, and took off. What for ? The others did not know. But they were curious, and in a few minutes the whole formation was again aloft. The curious ones came upon Pard at a place called Matariah. He was low, and flying round a felucca. He did all kinds of strange manoeuvres, that were closely watched by his fellow pilots " upstairs." Eventually he did the trick—the felucca suddenly heeled over and began to sink. Then, to show it was no fluke, Pard did it again—to another

THE NILE : FELUCCAS ; THE MOON ;
ROMANCE

felucca. Whereupon the others went into action, and "feluccaring proper" had been evolved.

At first, the new-comers achieved no success, and they too, had to dither above the felucca until they mastered the art. This is the correct technique as it was finally approved:—The pilot glides down-wind towards the big sail of the felucca, and at the very last moment makes a "split air" climbing turn to the starboard, at the same time lifting the nose of the machine and jamming on full throttle. Result No. 1—the slipstream of the propeller strikes the centre of the sail. Result No. 2—the sail shoots down to water, and the felucca starts on its way to the canal equivalent of Davy Jones's Locker.

This may sound callous—it probably was. But remember those were wild, high-spirited days, and in any case the pilots knew that the felucca folk could swim. Anyway, on that bright September afternoon, over a score of feluccas fell victims to the new-found sport which I have called feluccaring proper.

The Brass Hats did not describe it by the use of the verb, or the adverb, for that matter, but they managed to make their meaning clear. This must cease! It did.

Now for "feluccaring *de luxe*." As a matter of fact, the term "felucca" should not enter into this picture at all, as the craft which forms the setting of this story was not a felucca, but a dahabiya. This latter is the Nile version of a *de luxe* houseboat. A great, clumsy, junk-like affair, whose design and construction aim at utility, and not ornament. The

o

bigger ones had two comic-opera sails. But the main propulsion factor was the river current. Quite a *dolce-far-niente*-ish idea—you drift downstream.

"Yes, but what of the return trip?" you ask. For that, you get a tug.

I was introduced to feluccaring *de luxe* in this way: A service comrade of mine married the daughter of a Greek tobacco millionaire. In those days Greek was "colour" in the East, and whoever married "colour" was on the service "outer." None the less, my cobber married this new Helen, and I best-manned him. The marriage wrote finis to the bridegroom's military career; but his bride's family could not do enough for me. They were exceedingly—excessively—grateful. The bey's mansion at Cleopatra was open to me whenever I wished to, and could, stay with him. And he used to send magnificent parcels to me, when we were up the line. Eastern gratitude has to be experienced to be appreciated fully.

After the Armistice, pilots were encouraged, whenever possible, to fly before the populace, and thus encourage civil aviation. One afternoon I had flown to Luxor. It was very hot, and there was a baffling haze on the ground. I came in to the aerodrome cautiously. Everything would have been all right, had not a barraked camel, haze-hidden, got in the way. That cost the machine its under-carriage.

That evening in the main hotel, I was, in depressed solitude, trying to drink the nasty taste out of my mouth, when a waiter brought me a note. It was from the tobacco millionaire—would I join him

across the lounge ? Would I ? I forgot to tell you
that at the wedding, the bride's dress was garnished
with hundreds of real pearls, and that her dowry was
over £600,000. That will give you some idea of
what the wedding breakfast was like.

The millionaire said he was about to begin a
river trip to Cairo, in his dahabiya. Would I care
to come ? . . . The trip would take about three
weeks. That was a bit of a blow. Still, it was
worth trying. I wired brigade, and the next morning came the reply—" Leave approved." Promptly
the joyous news was passed to my host, and he told
me to be aboard at sundown.

After the wedding festivities and the Cleopatra
mansions, I was prepared for luxury on the dahabiya,
but nothing like what I was about to experience.
The moment I came aboard I had an embarrassing
shock. There was a house party of sixty-five, and
my kit, all of it in a haversack, was made up of one
clean shirt, pyjamas, shaving gear, and tooth-brush.
Also, I was the only Britisher. And the party
included thirty-seven ladies. What of the appearances ? That worry was soon dissipated.

My host came to my cabin. " How is your
wardrobe," he inquired, with a courtesy that called
for frankness. I told him. That will soon be
remedied, he said, and a little later a squad of
Indian tailors arrived, to take my measurements.
Next morning, they returned with the biggest swag
of clothes I've ever had in one issue—dinner-suit,
tails, mess-kit, whites, complete with all appurten-
ances. A small army of tailors must have worked

through the night. Then, and then only, we un-berthed. That is Eastern hospitality.

It was truly a *de luxe* craft. It had a crew of seventeen, and its three decks provided a degree of luxury that was wellnigh incredible to a wage-earning, little-travelled Australian. There was, for instance, a palm alcove in the dining-room where roosted a fine orchestra; a gold dinner service; glorious crystal, with table trappings in keeping; and, so far as personal service was concerned, you would have thought there was a waiter for every passenger. Even now my mouth waters at the thought of that food. And in my thick pate lurk Eastern fairies to remind me of the trip.

We would pull into the shore whenever there was something interesting to be seen. We would go inland on similar trips. Always, everywhere, a millionaire, and a thoughtful one, would wave a magic wand. I cannot remember whether we had a magic carpet; but there was everything else. That trip was almost a page out of a fairy-tale.

There was, however, some hard fact-facing at Assuit. With only half the trip completed, all my leave had expired. Well, they didn't know where I was; the war was over; and I realized that such a chance would never come again. " Yes, I'll go on, sir," I said to my host. I carried on, until three weeks later the dahabiya tied up at Kasser Nil wharf. Anyway, the music had to be faced, so I went to brigade headquarters. In the corridor I met a staff captain. " You *are* a beauty," he said.

" I know. Let's get it over. Where's the Old Man ? "

" He's in his office. And, you poor cow, he has a liver this morning. Cheero. See you at the killing."

The C.O. was busy writing, and did not look up for a minute or two.

" Oh ! So it's you ! Well, what have you to say ? You should be ashamed of yourself. You're a disgrace to your unit. Well, what *have* you been doing ? "

I had a brain-wave. " I know it's not done, sir, but I have a very good excuse which I realize would not be acceptable to every C.O. But the war is over and my record is clear. Suppose we postpone this interview until to-morrow morning, and you, sir, come along and dine in the atmosphere in which I have lived for the past six weeks ? "

" Um," snorted the Old Man, " an unusual request."

" Believe me, sir, I ask it with every respect. And, who knows but that this may be my last opportunity to ask anything of any one in the service ? "

The C.O. pondered the matter over. Then, being the sport he was, he accepted—on the understanding that neither his position nor his dignity would suffer through the acceptance.

" What time shall I call for you, sir ? "

" Seven o'clock. Will that do ? "

" Nicely, sir, thank you. Good morning, sir." I was whistling brightly as I passed the staff captain in the corridor.

" What's happened ? " he gasped. " Is the Old Man ill, or are you endowed with magic ? "

" I'll tell you later," I chuckled, as I hurried past.

Open throttle, per *gharry*, to the dahabiya. I explained my hastily-conceived idea to my late host. There was a gentleman for you. Of course he was agreeable. But madame, his wife, must be paid the compliment of having the refusal. We go to her boudoir.

" Madame, I have returned, as you see. I have reported to my brigade, and I've taken the liberty of inviting the Commanding Officer to dinner to-night."

" Excellent," said madame. " When does he arrive ? "

After that excellent reception, I put my cards on the table.

" If my scheme is successful, I will be free to re-join my squadron. If it fails, I may go back to Australia in disgrace."

Details were arranged. There will be a carpet across the wharf to the gangeway. The orchestra will be on the upper deck. The other guests will be hand-picked, attractive, entertaining, of status. As usual, dinner, wines, etc., will be in the hands of Hamid. I am to have the Rolls to pick up the Old Man.

" And," added madame, " I shall see that the saloon looks very charming for your English officer friend."

" Thank you, madame. I hope he is still my friend when I'm through with this."

At seven, to the minute, I drove the beautiful tourer up to brigade headquarters. " Come in," said the C.O. " You are at least punctual—on some occasions."

" Yes, sir, I am."

" Have a spot ? " . . . " Thanks." . . . " You'll find some Gold Flakes over there on the table."

Things moved nicely. When the C.O. had set the last touch to his mess-kit, I led him to the Rolls, and ushered him into the back seat, going round to the driving-seat myself.

Voice from the rear: " Excuse me, Mr. Sutherland, do you mind if I occupy the seat beside you ? " When I had graciously acceded to the request and the Old Man was seated, he said:

" I'm becoming extremely curious. Who happens to be the proud owner of this splendid car ? "

" All in good time, sir. We haven't very far to go."

But to heighten the mystery, I drove round Cairo, taking the longest possible route to the wharf. Naturally I was swanking.

There was quite a ceremonial when we arrived at the wharf. Friend Host met the C.O. at the foot of the gangway, and, after the necessary introductions, took his guest up to the top to meet madame. More introductions, and madame conducted the C.O. down to the saloon. There he met some eighty other guests, and after cocktails the party adjourned to the dining-saloon.

What a table ! Madame had excelled herself. It was a superlative meal. Afterwards there was dancing. At midnight, almost in Cinderella fashion I sneaked ashore and caught the 12.30 leave train. I had my original haversack, containing my army kit, and two big leather suit-cases, containing my river-trip kit. Next morning I reported to my squadron, from brigade, and nothing untoward happened.

Ten years later I met the brigade C.O. during one of the latter's official visitations within the Empire.

No, the C.O. could not recall me.

" Don't you remember, sir, an impromptu dinner on a dahabiya at Cairo in 1919 ? "

" Um, yes," dubiously replied His Nibs.

" Excellent crowd, weren't they, sir ? "

" Yes, delightful people. But really you have the advantage of me. You must tell me your name."

" My name doesn't matter at this stage, sir. But I owe you an apology. I failed to keep an appointment, sir, made for your office the morning after the dinner."

The Brass Hat looked very searchingly at me.

" You are not Sutherland, by any chance ? "

" That's my name, sir."

Whereat a broad grin broke across his puzzled countenance.

" Great Scott! Sutherland. What a delightful surprise ! Ever since that night I have always wanted to meet you, to thank you for a very happy memory."

We reminisce, having lots of interesting notes to exchange.

Then I came out of cover.

"By the way, I trust no irregular entry appeared in my confidential report with reference to my three weeks a.w.l."

"None, my friend. As a matter of fact, I was absent for five days myself ! "

The Brass Hat stood me a delightful meal. And told me of the wonderful trip he'd had with my friends on the Nile. That, as you have no doubt suspected, was feluccaring *de luxe*.

CHAPTER XIII

THIS chapter is fragmentary. When I confided to a journalistic friend that I was going to try to write a book, he gave me two words of advice. The first was—" Don't ! " Then, when that didn't register, he advised me (with an expression that said " The poor chap is still suffering from his crash ") to try to make the chapters of a uniform length. I gathered that all the best literary people did this. I, of course, am not one of the best literary people. Anyway, I have tried to follow this advice, but it has been very hard. With the yarns of any length, it was not so difficult. But when it came to the vignette-size incidents, well, that was a colour of a different horse. And this is that colour. Piebald, probably.

The first of these little yarns concerns " Peter " Drummond. My hero's real name is not Peter. Still, if you hunt through the current list of wing commanders of that name in the Royal Air Force and come to one with several decorations. . . . But that's another story. Peter was a " loot ' in No. 111 Squadron, R.F.C., when, in 1918, the latter was weaned from Bristol Bullets and D.H.2's to Nieuport scouts. This was a change very much for the better. The new machines were fast, had a very good climb, and could they dive ? The pilots were in ecstasies over them, but the Hun seemed to have inside information; he refused to come to close quarters. There were several minor clashes, but it was left to Peter to draw first blood. At least, blood is hardly the right word. However, judge for yourself.

Peter was a splendid pilot, a good shot, and he was always ready to mix it with the opposition. On this day he took off, climbed steadily towards the lines, crossed to the usual Archie accompaniment, and continued on over the enemy territory. He was watching the aerodromes and landing-grounds with more than usual interest, because he had a real machine, and he craved action. He got it some twenty miles or so behind the lines—a long way in those days. Above him appeared a formation of six Hun scouts, manoeuvring to attack. They came down on Peter from the sun, in what our American friends call a " power dive," their Spandaus streaking the heavens with tracer bullets. Peter turned under them and they zoomed up to regain height. More attacks, more getting hence by Peter, more zooms by the opposition. Then the Huns tricked Peter. Down they dived, and Peter again forestalled them; or thought he did. But as he flew clear, a burst tore into his engine—from under his tail.

One of the Huns had quietly flown away from his formation when the last attack opened, glided down, and then, as the opportunity occurred, climbed up under our friend's tail, giving him the aforesaid. With his engine spluttering and missing, there was only one thing for Peter to do, and he did it—went down, hoping for the best. The Huns flew in for the kill. But Peter was elusive, even on the " down grade." Several times he tried his engine, but to no effect. So there was nothing else for it, but Mother Earth, and whatever fate the German machines, or the land forces, were able to deal out.

Fate has a queer sense of humour. Just as the landing-wheels touched the ground on the Hun aero-drome at Tul Kerum, the engine cut in, and, with a roar, put its whole soul into the work. Off again sailed Peter, but with his Hun entourage in attend-ance. Sensing that their kill might slip through their aeronautical fingers his pursuers redoubled their efforts. Then, with the line still fifteen miles away, Drummond's engine cut out again. Nothing else for it. The distressed pilot put his machine down again. More bursts from the Huns. An-other run along the undulating plain—in actual distance a few hundred yards, but to the pilot it must have been a Marathon. And so the absurd affair continued like a Flanagan railway report—" off again, on again, gone again, Flanagan." Peter's flying hops averaged about a mile each, his enforced trundlings a few hundred yards, and all the time the irate gentlemen upstairs pumped lead. Not fruit-lessly (for at least they spurred Peter into some weird squirmings and twistings) but certainly without homicidal avail.

Paradoxically, the nearer the limping Nieuport got to home, the greater became the danger. For nearer the line were more Turkish troops, either en-camped or on the march. Hop, land, run, engine resurrection. Hop, land, run, engine. It was like a repeating decimal. And always the harrying Hun pack on his tail. Why they could not, or at least did not, hit this grasshopper is still a mystery.

But a crisis approaches. What's that ahead ? A camp—an enemy one, of course. Would Peter clear it ? No. Not a dog's chance. But, as he explained afterwards, he did not know the worst until he was right over this camp. Then, with the engine dead as cat's-meat, he plonked the Nieuport slap bang right into the middle of the camp, on the parade ground. Apparently the Turks were just as disconcerted as the visitor. They were resting, and, as was always the case in this event, there had been washings. Peter knew it only too well. For, while the Turks were milling and dithering about, he saw straight ahead of him, on the parade ground, a big clothes-line festooned with Jacko's laundry. Not that he worried about this, except as a possible minor obstruction ; he was chiefly concerned with getting his next hop under way. The engine opened up again and he rushed across the open space. Why didn't they shoot ? Well, in the first place, there wasn't time. Rifles would not be loaded—but all neatly stacked round the tent-poles; and the machine-guns, after the usual " spit-and-polish " of a rest camp, would have been in their cases. Further, it was only a matter of seconds. Down swooped the British machine; it ran across the parade ground; and then it was in the air again. It got away all right, but Peter felt a bump as he went over the clothes-line.

Hop, land, run, off.   Hop, land, run, off.   Still his Huns in attendance.   Only three of them by now, still pumping lead.   But the nearer Peter got home, the longer grew his engine bursts.   And then, when he was over the line, the worm, feeling mechanically better, turned . . . and fired a burst at its tormentors.   Whether it was the location, or the impudence of Drummond, I don't know.   But the fact remains that the Huns turned for home, and Peter came down.   And this time stayed down.   He then discovered the strangest streamer ever carried on the Eastern Front.   Twisted round the tail skid and the leading edge of the tail was about sixteen feet of clothes-line, complete with shirts and pants, " troops Turkish, for the use of."

No, the souvenirs were not used sartorially. This, for several reasons, chief of which was the fact that they were so poor in quality.

But Peter's tummy could not hold its last meal as efficiently as Jacko's line held the regimental duds. He was sick, very sick.   That a seasoned war-bird, in first-class physical condition, and with all the nerve about the place, should thus suffer is the best proof of what he had gone through.   When he was his own man again, he gave some advice, worthy of attention by civil as well as service pilots:

" Don't take the air without breakfast ! "

This is the story of our biggest " dog-fight " in the East.   Maybe I should write with an air of apology.   Because, compared with the shows on the Western Front, ours was piffling.   But it was only afterwards, when we swopped yarns with the Western Front pilots, that we learned the extent of their operations. In any case, I can still feel a quickening in the pulse when my memory takes me back to this scrap.

It took place at Amman, in 1918. Seventeen machines were involved—nine of theirs and eight of ours.

The show was not premeditated. We were not out looking for the Huns in quantity ; and vice versa. As I see it, the idea of war-time scraps is to get hold of a chap who is not expecting you, and do him a filth before he knows what it is all about. And the same applies to the plural. At least, that's my idea of it. This was one phase of the war in the air where chivalry was a.w.l.

Well, we met, the Huns in their Albatros D.3's and Pfalz scouts, and we in Bristols, and S.E.5a's. The formation commander signals " attack." After the initial dive, our formation becomes " column-of-lumps " immediately. It is every man for himself. We go hell-for-leather at those snub-nosed, black-crossed buses of the Hun, and they at us. The attack is simultaneous, and instantaneous. Our fellows are pulling their pound ; the Hun stands his ground. The air is pungent with the smell of cordite; filled with the guttural, staccato chatter of the Vickers, Lewis, and Spandau. Hectic work. Half-rolling, diving, zooming, stalling, " split-slipping," by inches you miss collision with friend or foe. Cool, precise marksmanship is out of the question. Albatroses, Pfalzs flash across your

ring-sights at terrific speed.   You press the triggers,
and the Vickers or Lewis sprays lead.   Your gunner, cursing horrifically, is shaking off a stubborn
Albatros from under your tail.

There goes old Jim in a spin.   Yes, it is a spin ;
no machine under control would behave like that.
Ah! There's a Hun snooping down to finish him
off, if he isn't already finished.   We'll get that
swine! Up, over and down.   Engine screaming,
flying wires wailing as we dive.   Thumbs down,
out   triggers.   A burst.   Rat-a-tat-tat-tat.   Another burst.   Rat-a-tat-tat.   God, will I never hit
him! Just let him stall again and I've got him cold.
Rat-a-tat-tat.   What's that ? Got him ! There he
goes in a sickening spin.   That evens it.   Up, up,
up—zooming up at 2500 feet a minute.

We rejoin the brawl above, to find it is still in full
blast.   Flashing, gyrating wing, stuttering streams
of lead, with only the tracer bullets, or a crackle or
smack in your wings or fuselage to apprise you of
where the enemy fire is going, or has gone.   A Pfalz
flashes by, and down, with a Bristol on his tail—
t-t-t-t-t-t—bullets thud into the tail of the Hun.
You can see 'em dotting, eating.   Almost as if the
pursued machine is voicing its anger and pain, the
scream rises louder and louder—the Hun zooms,
and turns in an endeavour to shake the Bristol off
his tail.   In vain.   There is a wilder, a more violent
noise.   The Hun machine is hurtling earthwards,
not diving or spinning.   Not trying to evade its
pursuer.   Hurtling . . . Finish.

Yes, I saw it—watched it.   Even in the heat of

A CAPTURED *ALBATROS*

CRASHED GERMAN PLANE IN BRITISH LINES,
PALESTINE

battle, there is an irresistible fascination about seeing a machine, ours or theirs, hurtling to its doom. Momentarily, at least, the doomed machine claims your attention.

The remaining Huns had had enough. They simultaneously turned north towards their aerodrome. This fight took place thirty-five miles on their side of the line—we couldn't afford to follow them. With one accord, and with throttles wide open, they were streaking for a cloud bank 2000 feet below, five miles to the north. We would have loved to continue the good work, but our petrol was low and Flight waggled his wings. That meant " form up." We counted the machines—seven. Jim was down, but we had got at least three of theirs. I am sure Jim would have felt satisfied, had he known.

All our machines were the worse for wear. Even from the cockpit we could see the holes, rents and tears in wing and fuselage; and " Snow's " engine was coughing out volumes of pungent black smoke. It was only when we were on the ground that we could learn the worst—or the best. But, after a thorough examination of our machines, we had another job of work to do, before we could refight the action in the best setting—the mess. That work was the filling in of the combat forms.

Now, fifteen years later, this filling in of combat forms seems to have been an extraordinarily cold-blooded business. Judge for yourself. The pilot had to state briefly the opposition, the type of enemy machine, its armament and belt make-up, and the

P

manner in which the engagement terminated. But
divil a word was the pilot expected to say about himself or his machine. He could have been wounded
nigh unto death—in which case, of course, it would
be unlikely that he was writing a report—his observer
could have been killed, as was the case on not a few
occasions ; his machine could be a wreck ; but
those details were not wanted. All the Higher Ups
required was news of the opposition—how he man-
oeuvred ; the guns he carried, and how they were
mounted ; the type of ammunition used ; and how
the enemy reacted to our pilot's tactics.

After all, this was just as it should be. The
squadron doctors, physical and mechanical, soon
learned of the ailments of personnel or aircraft ;
these were only of local importance. But data, such
as that furnished by the combat reports, would
provide invaluable indications of how a Fokker with
two guns could be best coped with ; or how a certain
mixture in a machine-gun belt was particularly effective ; and so on. Here is a typical report:

Date : 4/8/17.
Time : 1200.

Squadron: 67.
Type: B.E. 12.a
No.: 6329.
Armament : Lewis and Vickers Gun.
Pilot: Lt. Ross Smith.
Observer: Nil.
Locality: Sharia.
Height: 4-500.
Duty: Bombing.

First H.A. (i.e., hostile aircraft) was 2 seater, of Albatros type, with 1 gun firing forward and 1 back. He was above me and I got in a short burst with top gun. We then turned, met nose to nose, and I got in about 30 rounds with Vickers gun. We came together again, nose on, and H.A. put down his nose and made a right hand turn, enabling me to get in a good dive of about 40 rounds. He then made off with his nose well down, into his own archies at Sharia.

Returning to the formation, second H.A. was encountered, a single-seater with 1 or 2 guns firing forward. It had a yellow fuselage, and 1 dark green wing and 1 dark brown, on top sides. We met nose on and I got in about 20 rounds. H.A. made right hand turn, under my wing, and went straight off towards Sharia. Both H.A. used very distinct tracers.

R. M. SMITH, Lieut.

Can you beat that for dispassionately efficient information ? It only needed a festoon of red tape and a rubber stamp to achieve Public Service perfection.

As per instructions, the maker of the report made no mention of the parlous condition of his own machine, or of the two holes, one in each cheek, and the missing incisor—" x " marking the route of one bullet, ex H.A. As a matter of fact, Ross Smith, lieutenant, laughed heartily when he saw himself, complete with bandages, in a mirror. As a memento of this particular action, I souvenired the combat-in-the-air report, and took a snap of its writer.   The latter is opposite page 40.

This next story is told because it deals with a phase of the make-up of the Australian war-bird, a phase of his character which produced all kinds of interesting results.   That trait was his insatiable curiosity.   Why? How? I wonder! As, however, this book is intended to present stories of flesh and blood, and not to be a speculative treatise upon the relation of the Australian's character to the mighty turn of events in general, I shall get on with it and continue wondering later.

First, you want to bear in mind that, as results have demonstrated, the Australian as a soldier was permitted and equipped to indulge his curiosity more than probably any other Empire combatant. Governed by a discipline more elastic than the others, and with a rate of pay that gave him more scope for satisfying his curiosity when out of action, he delved deeply into the mysteries of whys and wherefores. Of course, this is a generalization.   But I do know that most of my comrades were thus afflicted, or gifted, whichever you please.   And the following is a typical instance.

The 14th A.G.H. at Heliopolis was a splendid hospital.   Everybody spoke well of it, and not a few of us, pining for sweet slothfulness, sheets, and a change in food and in environment, did our best to wangle an official and recumbent visit.   Also the 14th A.G.H. had the only Aussie nurses on the Eastern Front.   Thank the Lord, there were

R.M.O.s who could and would help ; who could close a humane eye to a sick-parader whose ailment was not quite within hospital range. But everyone who had been under the spacious roof of the 14th A.G.H. agreed that Colonel Sawers, although a splendid surgeon, was also, as C.O., a strict disciplinarian, and that he would not tolerate any funny-business, especially so far as pranks or practical jokes were concerned. He knew the Australian soldier—knew his propensities for mischief. The hospital had its work to do. Any one who interfered with it was due for trouble.

One of our flight commanders was a patient at " 14." He was a " dinkum " cot-case. Wounded in the leg. I know that the story would sound more convincing if I mentioned his name. But he is rather touchy on the subject of some of his unofficial exploits—so he shall be nameless. This chap had reached the convalescent stage, and was entitled to move about the hospital precincts. At first it was excellent to be able to visit old cobbers, also hospital inmates ; and there were now new faces, new walls, and other important things for a newly arisen patient to explore. Also, there were nurses.

He was always mechanically minded, this chap. His meanderings round the hospital often took him past the general switch room, whose big board controlled the electricity of the whole outfit. This was interesting. Very. And so, as the sun filtered through the windows, speaking of spring in far-off lands, something of the spirit of the early explorers

filled the soul of our wandering patient, glorying in
his newly-found freedom.

" Clever fellows, electricians," he mused. " I
wonder what would happen if I put all those nice
black handles down, instead of where they are ?
Must try that some time."

Back he wanders to his ward for morning tea, but
he cannot erase from his mind the thought of those
fascinating black handles.   Over hours and days it
becomes an obsession.   He is suffering a bad attack
of curiosity.   Also, he is recovering rapidly from his
wound.   One morning the doctor marks him for
duty;   he is to be evacuated back to his unit the
following day.   For the remainder of the day
curiosity tightens its grip.   The victim fights hard
until that evening—until an hour before " lights
out."   An hour to go.   That's not much.   Besides, it's very quiet. . . . I'll do it.   Must see what
happens.

He steals stealthily down the corridors and reaches
the switch-room.   No one about.   Good!   Which
shall I pull ?   This fellow here is the biggest, here
goes!

Black out.   A moment's eerie silence.   Then
yells for lights from all directions.   Especially from
the operating theatres.   Orderlies and wardmen
scurry about, candles and hurricane lamps eat into
the darkness.   Soon an electrician rushes to the
deserted switch room.   A few seconds later all's
well.

Yes, there is a moral to this story.   If you monkey
around with the main switch of a big hospital, don't

get all nobly repentant and confess—at least, not to
the C.O. Our offender didn't. That's why he was
able to rejoin his squadron next day.

This is the story of another of our officers, one
undergoing special training at No. 3 Fighter Training Squadron at Heliopolis. A story of an officer
who did tell. It was summer. Most of the
flying was done in the early morning—about daybreak. This particular young fellow-me-lad was
glorying in his conquest of the air. With the
Makers of Regulations enjoying their well-earned
slumbers, he decided to tackle a spot of hedge-
hopping. To make it more interesting, he chose
what looked like good " targets "—the camps and
building at Abbassia. Gaily he " shot up " camp
after camp, to the articulate rage of the awakened
troops.

Then, across the main road and out on the desert
showed up a long three-storied building, looking
very lonely in its desert setting. No telegraph posts,
trees, or cables. An excellent place to " shoot up."
Down he dives, and flies round the building, at the
level of the second story windows. Strange, all the
windows are open. And what's that ? Can't be!
Still, that's what it looked like. I'll make sure.
So down he swishes, and around the building.
Gosh! it was. What the deuce is this—a girl's
school? Every window seems to frame a female form.
It is, as I mentioned before, summer and early
morning. And those girls are dressed—as becomes ladies suffering acutely from the heat, and

about to step into a cool bath—well, they were not wearing their Sunday best.

Petrol was running low, but that pilot was a bright lad. He did not finish his reconnaissance until he had located the bath-room.

That building was the nurses' quarters of an adjacent hospital. If you hunt up the records of No. 3 Fighter Training Squadron, you will find that in two weeks of October 1918 there were more early " training reconnaissance " flights than ever before or since.

P.S. The " discoverer " of the nurses' quarters was an Australian.

Believe it or not, war is a grim business, and official instructions are in keeping. You know, I think we rather fail to appreciate the form of these official do's and don't's. Of course, everyone sneers or laughs about their bloodless frigidity ; but, supposing you wished to issue an instruction, could you pen it quite as dispassionately, as funereally, as do His Majesty's senior officers ? Could you wring the last drop of humanity out of the words as they do ? It requires a literary genius of a very special type to deal just so clearly and unemotionally with every phase of service life, on the ground and above it, on the bounding main, and beneath it ; every minutest phase of it, and every aspect of how one should act towards, or against, the enemy, comrades, civilians and oneself.

But I must get on with my story : it concerns an instruction that was promulgated on our front in

1917. It read something like this: " Pilots will avail themselves of every opportunity to attack ground targets and expend 75 per cent. of their ammunition on such targets."

The selection of the targets was left to the individual, but there were times when the Hun or Jacko would make the decision. However, it was not very long before pilots had their own pet targets, and the garden of fun was in full bloom. The laddie who took his job seriously at all times could not see anything funny in the regulation. His was a strictly business choice—ammunition dumps, horse lines, and camp. Others favoured that exhilarating pastime of " hedge hopping the sleepers "—shooting up the stations the while. That is more or less conventional work. You would find, say, 95 per cent. of the ground strafers thus engaged.

Two of the unconventional pilots greeted the new regulation with whoops of joy. For it gave them a chance of combining work with pleasure. Please understand this point: these chaps were, first and foremost, men at war; they were there to kill, and maim, and harm the people who would do the same to them, given the opportunity. But they had not reached that dreaded, dreadful stage when everything was done in grim seriousness. They could pump lead or unhitch bombs with one hand while with the other they waved a jester's staff. Well, judge for yourself.

Pilot A was always a close student of the daily Intelligence reports. He had discovered that when things were normal on the front—that is, when no offensive was in progress—the Turks always sent a train down towards Beersheba every afternoon; and this would be the only train of the day. Now, Pilot A used to expend his 75 per cent. of ammunition on this train. Just how much damage he did was never known; but many's the time Jacko's bully-beef was delayed.

Jacko would not take this kind of thing without doing something about it. So, as Pilot A soon learned, the train always carried a machine-gun mounted and manned in a truck. The moment the persistent Bristol swooped down, the train would come to a stop, and the machine-gun crew would blaze away.

But A soon found a way of beating that. He would dive full out, and then fly so low that the mounted gun could not be brought to bear on him, at the same time peppering the train. A few days after this tactical victory for the Australian, the Bristol dived down to have its usual strafe.

Immediately the train stopped; three soldiers sprang out and, carrying their gun, sprinted to a nearby knoll; there rapidly mounted the gun, and declared war. This was a colour of a different horse. Pilot A, however, was a quick thinker. Also, he admired guts, and those machine-gunners were not abdominally deficient. He did not " go " the machine-gun. Instead, he dived on the engine and gave the driver's cab merry hell. Off, up, turn, down, and another peppering for the driver and the fireman. These, the pilot could see, were decidedly uncomfortable. Eventually, after a few more dives, the engine crew panicked. Without a thought for the machine-gunners on the knoll, who were still tearing bullet-holes into the atmosphere, the driver opened the throttle and away puffed the train. Pilot A kept it going. He " spurred " it. And every time he put a burst uncomfortably close to the engine cab, the driver would " turn on " everything.

Only when the train reached territory that was too dangerous for the machine did Pilot A fly off—to see what had happened to the German machine-gun crew. There they were, still by their gun in the original position. And, as the plane approached the crew cut loose. The pilot did not return the fire. He saw that the gunners had no kit, he knew that it was going to be a bitterly cold night, and that they would not be picked up until next day. He waved cheerily to them and then flew home.

Pilot B had a rather macabre sense of humour. He had been doing a great deal of hostile aircraft work, and was fed up with playing aerial policeman. Any number of machines may constitute a patrol, and on patrol you were told where to go, at what time, and the height you were to fly. When you reached your patrol area, you relieved the other machines on the " beat," and flew up and down the area—up and down, up, and down, until, when your shift was up, another patrol took over.

Pilot B utilized the last quarter-hour of his shift in choosing his " shoot up " target. He had developed a " hate " for German staff cars—he blamed the German staff for lots of things, including H.A.P. (Hostile Aircraft Patrol). The staff cars

were usually 6o-h.p. Mercedes tourers.   In those
days all the roads in Palestine were dusty ones, and
the German cars invariably moved along them as if
their occupants were rushing to catch the last
train.

Up in the sky, Pilot B would watch for the tell-
tale trail of dust thrown up by the staff cars.   When
he had spotted one the game commenced.   Taking
advantage of sun, clouds, and anything else useful,
he would swoop down on the car, always from the
rear.   With all " taps turned on," Vickers and
Lewis, the pilot would rip lead all round the car.   As
soon as the driver heard the screaming dive of the
Bristol, he would step on it.   But the poor wretch
had no chance against a good pilot in a good machine.
The pilot would not shoot to kill.   Rather, he would
devil the driver into crashing the car—make him
leave the road, and, at full speed, go down a valley or
pile up into an embankment.

Cat and mouse stuff.   Leaves a nasty taste in the
mouth—for any one who has not seen what a German bullet can do to one of your friends.

Contrary to the general opinion of people who
have never been there, the Arabian Desert has its
rainy periods.   And when it rains out there, flying
and most other forms of martial action are not possible.   At such times officers of our squadron usually spent most of their time in the mess.   Cards
were popular.   It depended on how close, or how
far away, was pay-day.   Also at such inactive times,
members of other units took the opportunity to pay

calls, official and unofficial, to our squadron mess, then located at Mustabig.

On the wettest of wet Sundays, there came two almost-honorary members of the mess—Major Wilfrid Evans and Captain Henry Leahy, " iodine kings " both, from a Light Horse Field Ambulance, then stationed at Sabket-el-Bardawil. They were well known to us, and on most occasions were very welcome. Again the condition of one's pay-book was the determining factor: we knew the Light Horse thirst. This time the visitors were welcome. There was a joyous chorus from our fellows. But immediately upon his arrival, Dr. Leahy missed a particular pal.

" Where's ' King ' ? " he asked. Since King has a star role in this story, he had better be identified properly. He was Captain Adrian Cole, M.C.

" Where's King ? "

" Oh, he's got a boil," he was told.

" Um, where ? "

" On the left side of his face. An' it's a beaut."

" Well, let's have a squint at it."

Viewed from a distance, the boil was impressive, and Leahy confided to his fellow medico that he would do something about it.

" It *is* a beaut," he added cheerily. " I'll fix it."

" Oh, will you," snapped Evans. " I saw it as soon as you did, and remember, young feller-me-lad, that I'm your senior. Any boil-operating that's necessary, I'll do myself."

Leahy was both upset and determined. Wasn't King a bosom friend, a second brother ? Wasn't he,

Leahy, the greatest boil-carver on the Eastern Front ? And what the hell did seniority have to do with the operation ? It was skill, and not a crown on the shoulder, that was necessary. And hadn't he, Leahy, first inquired for King ?

" You, you scut, you didn't have the slightest interest in the unfortunate gentleman until you learned he was afflicted ! "

That was the beginning of a strenuous verbal brawl. We mere pilots and observers became embroiled—on both sides. Finally, when funds were down to bedrock—most of the argument had taken place in the mess—a Solomon came to give judgment. Why not toss for it, he suggested. Now that *was talking*. They tossed. Doc. Leahy won. *Exeunt* all.

We followed the winner to where King lay in his tent, cursing frightfully and completely unaware of the reason for the visit. Doc. Leahy broke the news. King was firm. And profane.

" Not on your life ! " he snarled, with bullocky trimmings.

Like a fond mother reasoning sweetly with her recalcitrant offspring, Doc. explained things.

" No ! " shouted King.

Doc. Evans was eloquent, in a martially bedside manner.

" No ! " roared King.

" Don't be a squib," chorused his fellow officers, among whom were Ross Smith, Murray Jones, Les Ellis, Bill Bowd, and Rex McNaughton. They implored King to be brave. They besought him to uphold the reputation of the squadron. They promised him a sweet after the operation. They pointed out to him the irremediable injury that might affect his classic beauty if he wasn't operated on. They demanded to know if any self-respecting Hun could be expected to fight a pilot of the squadron if this blot on its escutcheon—a hard word to say at that moment—was allowed to continue.

"No! No! No!" howled King, clutching his aching face.

"Well, it's got to be done," declared one of the pilots. "We poor —— have to live with you, and the sooner the —— thing is out, the better for the harmony and the revenue of the mess. Come on, you fellows, grab him, and cart him off to the hospital tent." No sooner said than done. The two doctors, smiling happily at the thought of a good deed to be done, brought up the rear.

The hospital tent was only of the bell tent pattern. As was the usual practice in a bomb-infested area, the tent was dug-in between two and three feet. The patient, smiling wryly, was more or less resigned to his fate, and by the time the doctors, orderlies, and spectators had crowded in, the tent was packed to capacity. Orderlies busied themselves, the primus stove was brought into action, the instruments laid out, and the doctors assumed a professional air.

"All ready, Doc.," said an orderly.

"Right," replied Leahy. "Bring it over here."

Squick. . . . K-K-K! Then crash! crash! The tent collapsed. Patient, doctors, orderlies, spectators, instruments, primus, blood all mixed up on the floor. It certainly was a mess. And the language! To make confusion more confounded (not to mention damned, blasted, and whatnotted!) no one could locate the door. At last someone did. With the door opened from the outside, we were able to sort people and things out. Never did any one look so dismal as poor King. But the boil was ruined. Nothing, and no one else, was. Truly a special providence had spread his wings over that tent.

But why had it collapsed? That special wing-spreading deity proved to be a pilot of No. 14 Squadron R.F.C., who had made a poor approach. His under-carriage had hit the top of the tent. As I mentioned before, it was the rainy season, and the guy ropes weren't exactly ready for a 70-m.p.h. whack. Why did it choose this particular tent? For further information apply (in vain) to Group Captain Adrian Cole, Air Board, R.A.A.F. and sometime chairman of the Melbourne Centenary Air Race Sub-committee!

At the conclusion of his England-Australia flight, Frank Chichester was asked by a friend of mine what was his worst experience.

" Well," said Chichester, with a glint in his eyes, " like all great pilots, I got lost flying south from Darwin. When I landed I drank some water from what I afterwards learned was a bore drain. . . . Have you ever had dysentery when flying ? "

One of our observers, who served in Palestine, could sympathize with Chichester. Chlorinated water had done all manner of unkind things to his

MAJOR YOUNGHUSBAND USUALLY WROTE A BETTER HAND THAN THIS. BUT
HE WAS ELATED AND VERY BUSY AT THE TIME HE MADE OUT THIS RECEIPT

innards. Ordinarily, he would have reported sick and would have been within easy reach of the place he so often required to visit. But Allenby's final advance was in its final stage. Every possible man was in the air, harrying the enemy to the Armistice. Well, this chap stuck things out as long as possible, but eventually his agonized voice begged the pilot to land. The pilot had known dysentery. He landed near Jiljilie.

The observer certainly had his sensibilities. There was no one within half a mile; and the plane ensured a certain degree of privacy. But he chose to go behind a nearby sand-dune. As he did so, a Turkish officer ran from the other side. The pilot whipping out his revolver, covered him, and ordered him to the machine.

Equipment and uniform showed that this was no ordinary officer. Also, he had a magnificent pair of Zeiss glasses (which, by the way, have since been levelled at many a race at Flemington and Randwick) and a haversack. The pilot could not identify the insignia of rank, but obviously this was too important a person to hand over to a mere Aussie guard, who might subject him to the indignity of being " ratted." Yes, that would have been too awful. Besides, the pilot particularly wanted to get to G.H.Q. So, with revolver as interpreter, the Turk was ushered into the machine, and parked at the feet of the observer (who was feeling much better, thank you), and flown to Ramleh. After being refreshed at the mess, he was taken to Richon (G.H.Q.).

Q

That visit supplied the Higher Command with
invaluable information, and the captor with a unique
souvenir.   The truth of this story is guaranteed by
the following exhibit :

Received from Lieut. Sutherland, R.A.F.,
Commandant Hakhi, Turkish Army and seven
packages of documents.

C. YOUNGHUSBAND,
Major.

General Staff,   G.S.
   Intelligence,
      20/9/18.

The information?   Well, that prisoner was a
corps commander.   He had been retreating with his
disorganized rabble, and the British attack had
pressed so quickly and powerfully that the officer's
staff had deserted him.   He was looking for some
conveyance when disturbed behind the dune.   And
he was so bewildered by the turn of events that he
had forgotten that his haversack contained comprehensive plans of the whole of the Turkish dispositions in that part of the world.

Apropos of field-glasses : I think one of the best
examples of mass souveniring in the East was put up
by an Australian—a Light Horseman.   Just across
the way from his own, was the camp of an English
mounted regiment.   A very " spit-and-polish "
outfit.   Very much parade-groundish, with bits and
stirrup-irons nickled and so forth.   Well, the Aussie

unit was due to be inspected by a general. The inspection took place, and the general heartily congratulated the C.O., officers and men on the smartness of their turnout. The C.O., however, was amazed at the change which had taken place overnight. He " tumbled," but he was a sportsman. Later the " borrowed " Tommy equipment was returned.

Ted Kenny was returning late from a reconnaissance. He was flying a " Harry Tate " and gliding in nicely when about ten feet above the ground, the pilot felt a terrific bump. That's one slight fault in an aeroplane: when anything goes wrong, you cannot stop and investigate. Well, Ted knew something drastic had happened, but, at that moment, there was no opportunity to investigate. The pilot went on and landed. Then his first glance revealed the extraordinary result of the bump —the plane, and its 140-h.p. R.A.F. engine had parted company.

How ? The Royal Engineers provided wrathful explanation. But what they said was a springscented zephyr compared with what Ted Kenny had to say. You see, the engineers had just run up a new telephone line across one end of the aerodrome. Quite an imposing work with twenty wires supported on posts. But Kenny was unaware of the show, and he had poked the nose of his " Harry Tate " smack into the wires. The impact tore out the engine by its roots, and the broken wires were unpleasantly festooned about the posts. Imagine how you would fare if, without your knowledge, a wire was stretched across your door and, face first, you walked into it.

We used to have smoke bombs for signalling purposes, and for ascertaining wind direction. They were innocuous affairs, and two of them were usually tucked down the fuselage at the rear of the observer's cockpit. One day one of our machines was returning from a bomb raid on Kutrani. It had been a hectic affair and the machine had been shot up badly from the ground. But the machine was mooching along nicely, until, about forty miles from Beersheba, the observer noticed a column of thick yellow-green smoke pouring out of the tail of the machine. Promptly he drew the attention of the pilot to the disquieting happening.

" Fire," yelled the pilot; switched off his engine and straightaway force-landed—in the desert. Standing orders decreed that in the event of a machine force-landing in enemy territory, the crew set fire to the petrol and completely demolished the machine, in case it fell into enemy hands. Promptly the crew set about carrying out the orders, but, before the petrol fire got into its stride, the other fire petered out. At least, no more smoke appeared.

Then, simultaneously, the pilot and the observer had a brain-wave—the now dead fire had not been a fire at all. Only one of the smoke bombs letting off smoke—a bullet from the ground had set it off. And while the master minds sadly reasoned things out, their own fire wrapped the machine in a death grip. Gone was their means of transport. Ahead, to home, was forty miles of desert. No food. No water. But an abundance of bitter thoughts, and many, many forceful words. Yes, the pair got out of the *consommé*. But never more was a pilot of our squadron tricked by smoke-bomb smoke.

It was a more than usually hectic mess night at Aboukir in July 1917. The mess held some two hundred odd pilots, observers, and "Huns." There was the usual talk of shop, and towards the exhilarating end of the evening, someone wanted to know whether it was possible to land a machine on the top of the hangars without injury to the pilot.

" Easy," yelled Murgatoyd. " I'll give it a go in the morning."

He was an instructor, and a favourite throughout the wing. And could he fly ! After the Armistice I saw him give an exhibition in a Bristol Fighter that was one of the most polished bits of flying I've ever seen. But to get back to the job.

At Aboukir there were streets of hangars, all linked one to the other. The roofs were of the ridge and valley type. You know—up and down. Well, before daybreak, " Murgy " wheeled out an old Avro. And in the cold-sober morning air, taxied her out to the far end of the aerodrome. Then round he came, opened up, took off, and, at a height of a few feet, came straight for the front of the hangars. About fifty feet from the tarmac he switched off, held her off, and then zoomed her up the face of the hangar, and plonked her slap on the roof thirty-five feet above the ground.

Then Lieutenant Murgatoyd daintily descended and went to breakfast a hero. But his smile was a trifle moth-eaten when the adjutant came up and said that the Station C.O. wished to see him at 9 a.m. Murgy was not smiling when he came away from the Old Man. It took nearly a week to get that machine down. There are still people asking " How are the landings, Murgy ? High or low ? "

CHAPTER XIV

THIS story should interest those lay people who have been wondering what the air part of the next war is going to be like. It is a gloomy subject, but a topical one. A race in air armaments is under way, and, judging by the way gas-masks have been used by the civilian population in the mimic air wars at Continental capitals, in the next major war gas is going to be used—especially from the air—extensively, drastically and frightfully. That may, of course, not be so.

But I do know what aircraft could, and did, do in the last big scrap. I saw them win one of the last rounds of a campaign; saw them carry out what was probably the most decisive air action of the whole war. It was the kind of stunt that every red-blooded flying man longed for; an open go for guns and bombs; a chance to revenge fallen comrades; an opportunity to thrash the enemy into defeat. Out there in Palestine, we had some ugly memories to spur us on: the gas used against the Canadians at Ypres; the *Lusitania*; our defeat on the Peninsula; and, closer home, the A.I.F. casualty list at Beersheba. Besides, there was probably not a man in the squadron who had not lost a relation, a pal.

At last there came the Big Show, this chance that we had been waiting for. And then? Personally, I felt sick, slaughter-satiated, remorseful. Most of those in the squadron felt the same way. For this action, which I am calling " Nine Miles of Dead," was not so much war as cold-blooded, scientific butchery. I feel sick even now when I think of it.

Gas, we are now told, is so potent, so controllable, that fifty tons of one type of it, launched by aircraft, could wipe out in twenty-four hours the population of a city of the size of Paris or Berlin. We are told that it can be dropped in bombs, sprayed from guns; and that some types are so deadly that gas-masks are powerless against their venomous invasion. We have all heard of aircraft that mount a one-pounder quick-firer gun ; of automatic pilots ; of planes small enough to be carried by submarines, and planes big enough to carry five tons of bombs. So it could almost be said that we had only bow and arrow equipment in the times of which I am writing. But we, who saw what could be done, what was done seventeen years ago, find our thinking caps weigh heavily when the subject is the war of the future.

It had been common knowledge on the Palestine front that Allenby would launch a great offensive in the early autumn of 1918—in autumn because he wished to avoid the extreme heat of late summer, and the heavy rains of early November. Also, the time chosen would catch the full moon. As this was to be mainly a mounted operation, the moon would make night riding possible.

The operation was divided into two parts : preliminary and effective. The British had been facing the Turkish troops on a fifty-mile front, running from a point twelve miles north of Jaffa south-east across the Plain of Sharon, then east over the Mountains of Samaria.   This range rises to a height of 2000 feet, and falls away to a depression 1000 feet below sea-level, where its line crosses the Jordan Valley and ends in the low foot-hills of the Mountain of Gilead.

Our line was at that time divided into three sectors : Sharon Plains (fifteen miles in length), Samaria (fifteen miles), and the Jordan Valley (about twenty miles).   The Turkish positions were strong. Their line ran through ideal defensive country, rugged and broken, and well served by good roads and railways.   The British XX Corps were holding the line opposite to the Turkish XX Corps, and our XXI Corps opposed by the XXII Turkish Corps.

Zero hour was ordered for dawn 19 September. Preparations for the opening of the offensive had been intense for weeks previously.   Thousands of troops, guns and material of all descriptions had been moved from the Jordan sector by night to the neighbourhood of Jaffa and Ramleh and secreted in the olive groves.   (You groundlings would be surprised to find how even big forces can be tucked out of sight of searching aircraft.)

At the same time, a huge bluff was carried out to cloak the secret movements.   It requires skill to execute grand-scale movements without being found out.   The Gallipoli evacuation was a striking example.   Allenby, like Munro, after Hamilton the *generalissimo* on Gallipoli, could cover his tracks. Many dummy camps were built, and canvas horses were constructed on the horse lines, whence, Arab-like, our cavalry had faded away.   But the best trick of all was used in connexion with cavalry " indica-tors."   In the Jordan Valley it was something like " everywhere that Mary went, the lamb was sure to go " : everywhere there was cavalry, there was dust. So, although the cavalry had gone, the dust had to hang about.

The deed was done in a most ingenious way. Big, clumsy affairs, like harrows, and big baulks of timber, were dragged about the country-side by Fordson tractors and teams of horses.   Unless you have been in the Jordan Valley, you have no idea of the extent, and the density, of the dust-clouds raised by the movements of cavalry regiments.   These dust-clouds were visible to aerial observers up to a height of 8000 feet.   So you see, the dummy clouds had to be impressive ; otherwise Jacko would surely have scented a rodent.

That was not all.   For the benefit of the enemy Intelligence—which, so far as this operation is concerned, was rather flatteringly named—Allenby sat himself down in the Fast Hotel in Jerusalem. Staff, red brassards, " dogs-on-the cushions," sentry boxes, "posh " goings and comings.   All this, too, was a blind.   Allenby and his staff were twenty-five miles away at Richon.

The Flying Corps had had a busy time.   The opposition Intelligence may have fallen down on its job, but our winged Hun friends had eyes just as keen as ours.   They had to be kept from seeing things.   Our job was to drive the Hun out of the sky. We did it. For eight days before the offensive opened, not one German machine crossed the British lines.

The Turkish Command, however, did know that something was "a doing of." But, as was subsequently learned, he expected the blow to fall in the Jordan Valley. The dust-makers and the dummy G.H.Q. had done an excellent job of work.

Allenby planned to effect a breach of the Turkish line in the Plain of Sharon ; throw his cavalry through the breach, seize the plain, and cut the communications of the enemy, which all traversed the Esdraelon Plain, biblically yclept the Plain of Armageddon. This done, the Turkish Army on the other side of the Jordan would fall into our hands. So reasoned Allenby. The artillery barrage was to smash the trenches, and let the infantry make the breach in the line through which the cavalry was to gallop to cut the communications. Gallop is the word, for the communications were fifty miles away and they had to be dealt with before nightfall of the first day.

An operation of this nature gives one a new appreciation of what is involved in good staff work. There were six divisions of troops engaged. They had to move faster than ever troops had moved during the war. They had to have food, water, ammunition, medical attention. I cannot explain how the job was done. If you are inclined to dismiss that achievement cheaply, think how often you have messed up packing a picnic hamper or a suit-case, and then use your imagination in a giant war setting.

The Flying Corps had made a good start.   Our next job was to keep the Hun airmen out of the picture—to prevent them from knowing what was really happening when the offensive opened.   We felt confident.   But, when the Wing Commander, Colonel R. Williams (Borton had been promoted to Brigadier-General and the command of the Palestine Brigade) explained to us our part in the operation, its magnitude caused an unusual quiet.   On the afternoon before the show, Dicky called all the officers of the squadron together in the dining-tent of the mess.   He explained things with his usual incisive thoroughness.

As the story unfolded the faces of the listeners showed how they were affected.   Oliver Lee was sitting opposite me.   His grin seemed to say : " Now, here's the big chance with my double Lewis." Alister Kirk's eyes wrinkled : " I'll never miss 'em now that I'm used to those stocks on my Lewis guns." Nunan was wondering if he would have the chance to repeat his sledge-cum-dynamite bombing act. Tonkin's face was a study.   But we all could guess his thoughts.

By the way, about this unique idea of Nunan's. For months we had been trying to bomb a certain railway viaduct.   We could hit it, did hit it on several occasions ; but our usual bombs, such as the 112-pound Hales, and the 20-pound Coopers, were ineffective.   Nunan had made many attempts, but his punches lacked power.   He was exasperated. But, as indicated in previous chapters, he was nothing if not adaptable.   So he schemed a scheme.   The flight carpenters and artificers were requisitioned, and there was lugged into the hangar one of the weirdest gadgets ever seen there.

It was a heavy wooden affair, like a sledge—the kind of sledge with which country people haul their milk in winter. The idea? To use it as a carrier for two hundredweight, of dynamite fixed on the fuselage, and, flying low, drop it on the recalcitrant viaduct.

The gadget—we could not evolve a name for it—caused a lot of merriment. But Nunan was not only in earnest ; he also was a " hot " engineer. He arranged for slabs of dynamite to be strapped along the top of the Whatsit. Fusing was a workmanlike job. There was a cord attached to the fuses and to the machine. When the " bomb " was dropped, the dislodgment of the machine-end of the cord was to ignite the fuses, and up would go the viaduct. Special fittings were necessary to attach the thing— Lord ! I wish I could think of a name for it—but Nunan designed and made them all. Also a special quick-release gadget.

When the whole thing was finished, it was im-pressive-looking in a Heath Robinsonesque kind of way. As was the case when " Agnes " was built, only two doubts remained. First, could Nunan lob the business on the viaduct ? Second, would the fuses set off the explosive ? The inventor proved that he was still an excellent marksman—he put his unique " pill " right down the " fairway." But the fuses fell down on the job. The viaduct stayed in one piece. However, Nunan was prepared to try again—hence the expression on his face as he listened to Dicky.

Before returning to the main story, I had better explain, too, Tonkin's pet stunt. He had an insatiable curiosity with regard to lethal weapons in general, and Mills bombs in particular. At any time, Mills were nasty things. Thank God, they were not designed for use by aircraft. But Tonkin had his own views. After a lot of back-yard research he evolved an even stranger device than Nunan's bomb. It was more or less impossible for a pilot to handle Mills bombs from aircraft—two hands are not sufficient to handle the aircraft controls, pluck out the bomb pins, and then hurl the bombs. So, Tonk staggered into the hangar one day with an extraordinary affair that looked something like an outsize in the Pipes of Pan. He called it a " Mills battery." The pipes, four of them, were six-foot lengths of roof down-pipe. The inside diameter of the pipes was just wide enough to take a Mills.

Tonkin explained the workings. Each pipe would take fifteen bombs—that made sixty Mills per " battery." At one end, the pipes were sealed.

Yes. Yes. We could see that. But we were very sceptical. How, we asked, would the Mills be dropped, and how would the dropping be controlled?

" Comparatively easily," he explained. The sealed end of the battery was to be fitted on to the rear spar of the wing, alongside, and parallel to, the bomb racks. The open end faced the front. In normal flight, the pipes would be more or less level.

There was an arrangement of hinges and spiral

springs whose details I shall not try to explain. But to drop the Mills Tonk just pull a lever, so— and the Mills would drop out.

" But what about the pin ? " we asked. How would it be operated ? The pin, you see, does the same for a Mills bomb as the cock does for a rifle or a revolver.

" Like this," he triumphantly replied. " Something was necessary, of course, to hold back the handle of the bomb until you wanted the damn thing to explode. Well, I've solved the problem by using parchment. You bind a strip around the handle, and make sure it is firmly held by fixing and binding with a dab of special glue. Then you may pull out the pin without fear of the hereafter. When the Mills is dropped on its target, the parchment bursts, the handle is released and—bang ! How's that ? "

It sounded all right, but the battery looked so fantastic that we chaffed Tonk unmercifully. He took it all, and set about building another battery. This, too, was fastened to the plane, on the opposite wing.

Tonk had finished making his batteries, and had tested them to his satisfaction, just when Dicky gave us the news of the coming offensive.

Dicky quietly told his story, expressed his full confidence in his old squadron, and wished everyone " Good hunting ! "

It was startling, as well as exciting news. We talked it over. What would the Huns do ? Would they put up some sort of a scrap ? Then we remembered that Dicky had stated that the No. 111 Squadron were to keep a continual patrol over the Hun aerodromes, with orders to bomb any machine attempting to get off, and to shoot down everything in the air. A few months earlier that order to 111 would have seemed absurd ; it would have taken much more than one squadron to keep the Hun ground-bound. But at this time, the Hun, like Jacko, was very much the worse for war. So, all things considered, there was not much likelihood of our striking trouble " upstairs." But there should be lots and lots doing down below.

While we were talking targets—and all of us had favourites—one pilot voiced an interesting idea :

" Well, chaps, if I am going to have an open go, I'll use only common and tracer, about five to one. No use wasting incendiary and Pomeroy. And I'll carry another four or five drums."

" Go on," retorted a cynic. " So you're going to be Executioner No. 1 of the squadron, eh ? And, pardon my stupidity, but where *are* the targets coming from ? "

" Jacko will put up the fight of his life, and don't you forget it," chimed in another.

We were still jabbering excitedly when the flight commanders came into the mess. They had received further news and instructions from Dicky. They, the Flights, looked serious. No social visit, this. Our pow-wow broke up. Soon each flight was called together by its commander. Instructions were explicit. This point was emphasized— things *must* go right. Then to the hangars to check up everything checkable.

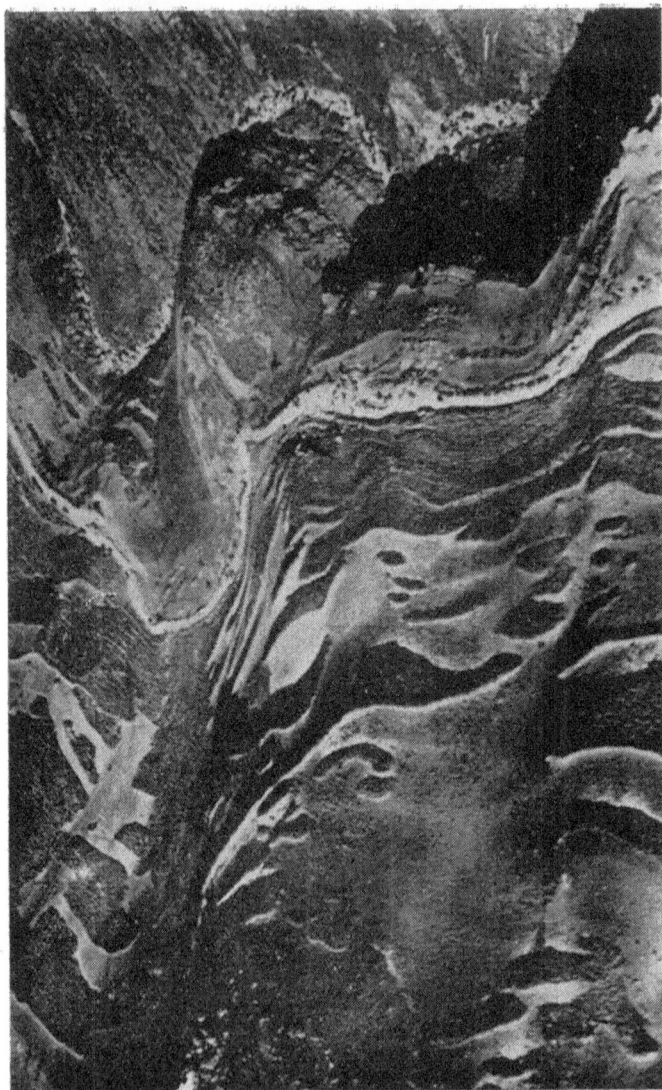

NINE MILES OF DEAD

Everyone was keyed up. Never was ammunition so closely looked to. Every round was closely
scrutinized for deep set caps, bulgings, thick rims,
separated cases. Then the rounds that were passed
were all given the once-over with metal polish, to
assist them to slip easily into the feed blocks of the
guns. Extra drums were filled and additional
belts. Every man jack in the squadron worked
flat-out to be ready for the curtain-rise on 19 September. But for all the importance of the occasion,
the spirit of fun that so often danced merrily in the
hangars was soon in evidence again. As usual, the
pilots and observers got into many good humoured
verbal holts.

Tonkin was a human dynamo. He fussed and
fussed with his batteries. This was to be his chance.
He would show what he could do, now there were to
be the right kind of targets. We gave him hell.
But the bloodthirsty cow was too busy, too happy, to
be offended.

I forgot to mention that the gunnery in the squadron had always been exceptionally good. For
months past we had practised at every opportunity.
Thousands and thousands of rounds had been fired
on the squadron range; and there had been sterner
practice a-plenty in action. Equally important, we
had never neglected opportunities to improve ourselves at clearing gun stoppages. After all, it did
not matter how good a shot one was if one's gun
jammed and stayed jammed. That was an experience few were able to discuss.

The country in which we were to operate we knew

R

thoroughly—knew it better than our home town or district. We had carried out numerous recos over it. We did not need our maps or photographs to refer to. When you have spent many hours methodically cruising over an area, it registers.

At dinner that night there was a feeling of tension, of restlessness. Again we talked of targets. Talked and talked. But not over drinks. Mustn't be any thick heads or shaky hands next day. What the deuce *was* going to happen ? Some brooded ; some wrote letters—you could tell by their air that this might be the last word to their dear ones. Nearly every one bought extra cigarettes and chocolate. Handy things, those, if one is forced down in the wrong place.

Bed early. Shortly after midnight there was an orderly bustle in one hangar. Soon the biggest plane on the front roared into life. This was the first and only Handley-Page that had come our way. Two Rolls-Royce engines. Ross Smith was the pilot, and, as was only fitting, he was going to set the ball rolling. His job was to bomb headquarters of the Turkish 7th Corps—at Nablus. He carried sixteen 112-pound bombs. That raid succeeded. Especially in one important particular—the telephone exchange was wiped out. No. 144 Squadron did the same at Afule. A promising start.

At 3.30, an hour before dawn, the squadrons were awakened. Breakfast, and then to our flights. At 4 o'clock we took the air. Dawn was just showing in the east. The earth was a dim, dark mass; not a light showing anywhere. A perfect morning. So

peaceful.   But we knew the intense activity that
was taking place on one side of the line.   How we
hoped that Jacko was unsuspecting!   I nearly wore
out my wristlet watch.   But, punctually to the
second, hundreds of guns, big and small, flashed into
action.   Even from our height of 10,000 feet the
sight was magnificent.   We could not hear the guns,
but we could feel the percussions.

At the outset there was an encouraging sign: the
Turkish artillery had not immediately replied.
That proved they had been taken by surprise.   No
work for us yet.   We had to wait until the barrage
lifted.   Then, when our infantry went into action,
we had to find out whether the Turkish reserves
were being rushed from the neighbourhood of Tul
Kerum to reinforce the line.

As suddenly as they had begun, the British batteries ceased fire.   We were too far away, and too
high, to see the infantry move forward.   But soon
long, black lines were to be seen moving northwards
through the Turkish positions.   Great! That could
only be cavalry—our cavalry.   Moving fast, too,
and towards Tul Kerum.   Obviously, the artillery
and the infantry had won their first rounds.   Allenby's " ride " had begun.

Now we were in the picture.   British machines
were everywhere, each with a pre-arranged task.
No sign of the Huns.   No. 111 was doing its job.
We could see the artillery co-operation machines
mothering their batteries on that portion of the line
not yet engaged in the advance.   But it was 5.30,
and we had an appointment.   We had to meet a

bombing party bound for El Afule.   We met.   We did the job.   At El Afule there was a large working party trying to clear up the damage caused by No. 144 Squadron.   We decimated the one, and increased the other.   Other British squadrons were busy at work there.   This was bombing *de luxe*. No opposition upstairs. Archie bombed, or machine-gunned, out of action.   Perfect weather. We chose our own altitudes.   The targets could not be missed.   Railway station, aerodrome, material and dumps were blown to blazes.

Only when our loads were used up did we cease. Then back to Ramleh for another load.   And how we hungered for news as to the left!

We had been in W/T touch with our aerodrome. They were waiting for us with hair-trigger keenness. As soon as we landed a splendid crew took over. Mechanics on the engines, petrol and oil whipped in, mechanics filling the bomb racks with 20-pound Coopers.   Armourers at the front guns, testing, filling the belts.   Riggers going over the wings, tails, looking for bullet-holes or defects.   Orderlies on the tarmac with coffee and sandwiches, lighting your fag, putting chocolate in the pockets of your Sidcot.

" How are the stocks, Alister ? " (He had special stocks fitted to his gun.)

" Good!   But I fired only 600 into the railway station.   Wait till I get a real target. . . . Any one seen Tonk ? "

" No.   He's out on patrol and without his bat-teries—those so-and-so pipes of his are no good at

12,000 feet.   But I'd sooner he had 'em than me.
Imagine what will happen him if Archie shoots away
some of that parchment business ! "

" Here comes Fin and Alan Brown.   They look
very happy about something—Too bad there's not
time for Fin to advise Allenby what to do now."

" Hey, Fin! See any targets ? "

" No, nothing unusual, yet.   But there will be in
another hour or so, and then tons of them, or I'm a
Dutchman.   Brownie and I'll find 'em."

Not much news from the left.   But apparently
the attack was successful.   " Stand to! " calls the
Flight Commander.   A last puff at the gasper.
Sandwiches are stowed away; we'll finish 'em upstairs.   Off on the second flip, feeling good.   This
time we'll see some real war.   And targets.

Over the Sharon sector we found them.   First a
Turkish column, cavalry and transport, retiring at
a gallop from the direction of Et Tire, towards Tul
Kerum.   About 2500 men and 500 vehicles; and
farther back towards the line there was another
column—between 3000 and 4000 infantry.   We
gave the cavalry our bombs.   From a height of 1500
feet.   We blew them to blazes.   Then zoomed on
the infantry and chopped them to ribbons with our
guns.   We couldn't miss.   Emptied our belts and
drums.   The poor devils were panicky when we
first dived down, but they tried to drive us off with
rifle and machine-gun fire.   No use.   We left off
only when our ammunition was exhausted.   The
Turkish survivors were in disorderly flight all over
the countryside.

Back to the aerodrome to load up and refuel. Out again in ten minutes. More targets this time— Guns and bombs, triggers and bomb-toggles. Home again, out again—t-t-t-t-t-t-t. Crash ! Crunch ! Crash ! Targets ? We couldn't deal with them all. A day of slaughter. Only when nightfall came and, gathered in the mess, we told of our individual experiences, did we realize the full extent of it. And how had we come out of it ? Wonderfully. Our only real casualties were Tonk and his observer, Clinnie. They had been shot down and taken prisoners by the Turks. But before Tonk had had time to even offer his captors a fag, one of our cavalry regiments swept on the scene, and the few Turks who escaped did not have the prisoners with them.

Came more news. The 7th and 8th Turkish Armies were in full retreat. They'd be there for us next day. No doubts as to targets now. We knew. Things were lively in the mess.

Ross Smith again set the ball rolling that night. Away roared the big Handley to Jenin. Targets— the railway station, and the big aerodrome. They received two full loads: bull's-eyes.

Extraordinary as it may seem, next morning (the 20th) found the situation unchanged in the Eastern or Jordan sector. The Turks there seemed unaware of the catastrophe that had befallen their 7th and 8th Armies. The remnants of the stricken armies were streaming into Anebta, Sibusti, and Nablus.

The dawn patrols brought news of an abundance

of targets.   Our first raids were on the retreating
Turkish columns on the Afule-Samaria road.   It
was butchery.   Troops, disorganized, nervy and
dispirited, had no chance, no protection against
aircraft that could dive on them at 160 m.p.h.   The
Turks blazed away with their rifles, and the machine-
guns went into action.   But we were too fast, too
elusive.   And the pilots were two-handed fighters.
The right hand was free for the bomb-toggles; the
left was sufficient for flying, and simultaneously
firing the Vickers.

Those German machine-gunners were men.
There were several squads of them in the column.
They did not flee.   They went under, in action, at
their guns.   We learned later from other units,
flying and mounted, that the Germans always fought
to the last man.

Those columns were eventually blocked by the
masses of dead and wounded.   We took a terrible
toll.   Only when the belts, the drums, and the
bomb-racks were empty, did we leave—for more
ammunition.   And there was another scourge for
the retreating Turks.   The Light Horse were on
the job.   Those lads were moving faster than ever
before.   This time, there was no gallant, determined
enemy to bar the way.   Only broken, dispirited
mobs that usually surrendered at sight.

It was sheer butchery.   The Hun was out of the
sky;   the enemy anti-aircraft batteries were either
captured or in full retreat.   There was no need for
pre-offensive heights.   We flew just high enough
to keep clear of our bomb splinters.   That was

about 150 feet.   Child's play for those in the air.

Late that day, the second of Allenby's push, fires broke out at Balata and Nablus.   They gave the alarm to the Turkish forces around Lubban and across the Jordan.   The Turks moved hurriedly to the rear.   But in vain.   We could see the movements.   Weary sheep have no chance against the eagles.

It was a gloomy night in the mess.   Gone our excitement of a few days previously.   Gone the elation of having Jacko just where we wanted him. Targets ?   No one wished to discuss them.   We were weary of slaughter.   On the trips to and from the aerodrome there was time for thinking—too much time for the kind of thoughts we had.   Most of us had been ten hours in the air on each of the two days.   We should have been too tired to think. But there was a dreadful thought in many of our minds—the butchery had just begun.   We knew that the retreat was going to develop into a rout. And then, what ?

For all our mental sickness and turmoil, we were soldiers.   A duty, a vitally important duty, had been given to us.   For the first time in the war, we, the newest arm of the service, had the most onerous work in a major operation.   We were not going to fall down on our job.   But oh, those killings ! . . . Thank God for a bath.   That helped—it seemed to wash some of the invisible blood off our hands. Only the lucky ones slept that night.

Tonkin was with us again—it had taken him a day to get back to the squadron.   He had missed

the second day's action. His " batteries " were yet
to be proved. He spent most of the night in fitting
them to a new machine.

Dawn again—dawn of the 21st. One of our
first machines to get away was the Bristol manned by
Brown and Finlay. They flew out to see what was
happening to the east of Nablus. Their wireless
soon crackled news. The enemy's transport and
artillery were attempting to escape along the Ferweh
road, which, on the east, ran to the Jordan. That
was sufficient—our first formation left for the
scene.

This was a rugged, barren country-side set in
black basalt hills. They were not very high, but
they were steep ; most of them were unscaleable.
The road followed the floor of valleys. Passes
would be a better term. We were soon there.
We had come to a bomber's, a machine-gunner's
paradise. A giant, greyish-black snake, nine miles
in length, was sprawled beneath us—sprawled
tortuously this way and that. It was not moving
forward. Brown and Finlay had seen to that.
They had attacked and battered the head—it could
not move forward. A few moments after we arrived
it could not move back. We saw to that. The
first machine had bombed and machine-gunned the
transport at the head of the column. We did the
same to the tail.

Have you ever seen a traffic jam in a one-way
street ? One carrying wheeled traffic, motor and
horse ? Imagine what would happen if two or three
cars at the head of the stream caught fire, and they

with full petrol tanks.   Unpleasant, eh? Especially
for the vehicles immediately behind the blazing cars.
Now open your mental eyes and tune your mental
ears.   The wheeled traffic is still there.   But there
are also thousands of men marching ; they are
carrying heavy packs ; they are tired, dispirited.
Now substitute steep hill-sides for the buildings.
And instead of those blazing cars at the head of the
traffic stream, visualize ten, twenty, wrecked,
smashed lorries, heaps of struggling, maddened
horses, and, in the vehicular debris, piles of dead and
wounded men.

Look up now.   Overhead, close enough for you
to see the goggled faces of the crew, is a diving
machine;   three guns pumping lead.   Yes, you can
even see some of the bullets—they're tracer.   And,
Great God, they're coming at you!   And you can
see little balls hurtling down—balls that are bombs.
Crash !   How they burst !   And those splinters from
the rock!   Whang!   Whang!   The vicious red of
the burst bomb, the kicking dust and the wheeling
smoke ;   the tang of the cordite.   The shrill agony
of maimed horses ;   the cries, the shrieks of your
comrades.   Remember, you're one of those poor
devils in the " street."   And you're up near the top
of the traffic stream.   What do you do ?   Which
way do you turn ?   Would you listen to the orders of
your officer—if he gave orders—if you could hear
them ?   Would you try to press forward, to get past
that ghastly, ever-growing pile-up ahead ?   Or try to
fight your way through that mad pressing mass of
lorries, guns, wagons, horses, oxen, and men forcing

you forward ? Climb the hill-side ? Lie down ? Take your choice.

The Turks had either experienced air attacks *à la* Allenby offensive, or they had heard what they were like from our victims of the two previous days. There was a panic at the first aerial onslaught.   It was only a narrow road, pinned in by sheer walls of rock.   At the head of the column those immediately behind tried to press forward. Impossible. Wrecked vehicles, bodies blocked the way.   And always the wreckage and the carnage continued. Let me put it another way—you find a big snake in a confined space.   You drop a big rock on its head, then another big one on its tail.   It is a very giant of a snake, but the two blows prevent it from getting away.   The coils move in agony, but they cannot thresh their way clear.   You stand above it and batter and batter it until. . . .

It had been butchery on those two previous days. But I can think of no word to convey the dreadfulness of this action.   As our bombs rained down, scores, hundreds of motor lorries, guns, and wagons were literally lifted off the road and smashed to pieces.   Our guns sprayed lead, never ceasing until a belt or a drum was empty.   Frantic groups were all the time rushing from the road, milling about, striving to get anywhere that might give some protection against this rain of death.   Many did get away from the road, but from upstairs we could see every movement.   We would dive, guns blazing or the Coopers hurtling.

The news had gone back to other squadrons.

Our gigantic target, we learned subsequently, was the remnants of the 7th and 8th Turkish Armies, with the bulk of their artillery, transport, and technical services. None of our land forces were closer than twenty miles. Alone, we had to deal with a force that outnumbered us by thousands to one. This was the Air Force's war. And what a hateful war it was. We were flying at a kind of " eye-drop " range above the road. From that height one could see the expressions on the faces of the poor devils below; could read the agony and the anguish in front of the gun-sights. One second it would be a team of horses: the next a bloody mass of shattered legs and carcasses. Here was a lorry with a mob of men milling about it. Crash! Lorry and men were whirling fragments. The pilot could not see immediately the destruction he had wrought. He had passed over it. But he could see the effect of the gun-fire and bombs of the machine ahead of him.

Tonkin's batteries were a terrible success. The pipes and the Mills functioned as he had planned. Ask any footslogger what a Mills can do to good targets—a nice group of close-packed soldiers. Ask him what would be the effect of sixty Mills, dribbled out at two second intervals over a solid mass of troops, hemmed in by walls of rock.

And Nunan's sledge! This time the fuses did work. Can you visualize the effect of half a ton of explosive dropped direct on a compact mob of men ?

In parts, the road was flanked by ravines, hundreds of feet deep. Here, the bursting bombs often lifted the smashed wagons and guns off the road and down into the dark depths below.   Here, too, the poor devils of troops tried to seek cover from the ravine sides.   In vain.   When the falling debris did not punch them down, the observer's gun-fire brought about an equally terrible death.

Ordinarily, the observer could not engage the same target as the pilot.   The pilot was shooting to the front and down, and loosing his bombs straight down;   the observer's field of fire was to the flanks, down and up.   In this instance the Turks on hill-sides, or down the ravines, were easy marks for the observers.   Irrespective of what the pilot was doing, there were always targets for the twin Lewis in the rear cockpit.

Some of the Turks did scale the hills.   Then, in desperation, they sniped our machines with rifle fire.   No good, poor devils.   They were brave, but they were driven out.   As a matter of fact, this sniper hunting was a welcome diversion.   At least, there was something remotely approaching a fight in this.   Below, on the road, and in the ravines, it was one-sided slaughter.

I saw a British machine down on a hill-top.   The sight came almost as a surprise.   Somehow it seemed as if we fliers were sacrosanct, beyond danger. Rifle fire, machine-gun fire, these were mere baga-telles when we remembered the days when the Hun was also in the air—the days when you got your man or your objective only if you were the better man or could pick your way through the Archie barrage. Even in the stress of butchery we had thoughts like these; afterwards, we talked of them painfully, in the mess.

What brought that machine down? I don't know. But when we flew over the crew were standing by it. Their cheery wave indicated that they were all right, and not even concerned. That attitude was a striking indication of the condition of the Turks. There were thousands of them. Here was an enemy machine delivered into their hands. And they did nothing.

At no time after the column was bottled up were there fewer than six machines over it. The others were either sprinting back to their aerodromes for more fuel and ammunition, or returning with further loads of destruction.

About midday we could discern a change in the attitude of the Turks. Previously, they had blazed away or striven desperately to escape up the hill-sides. Now they seemed to be resigned to their fate. White cloths and flags were waved in surrender. But, even if we had wanted to accept it, how could aeroplanes capture ground troops?

We scotched that snake on the 21st. We came back and further maimed and battered its coils next day. Yes, it was still there. We knew it could not get away—knew the road was impassable either way, and that the survivors could never beat those desolate, heat-wrapped, waterless hills. This was a rout. There were no lines of communication. No water, no food. Nothing. Why try to escape? Death was the easy way. . . . We were very obliging.

There were no medical supplies, and probably no

medical people. Both had gone the same bloody way. Out there, with the heat and the dirt, and the blowflies, gangrene and tetanus must have held high festival. We knew, from our own experience, that a wounded man left in the open without attention for a few hours would be fly-blown. These wounded Turks were in the open for over two days. No—no wounded, under those conditions, could have lived that long.

The 22nd. Raid. Bomb. Guns. 'Drome. What do you do when you haven't the facilities to capture big bodies of the enemy who want to surrender ? Leave them alone ? Wave them a cheery greeting ? Don't be silly. *You* don't know your war. Many of those poor devils were killed a dozen times over.

The bombs continued to rain down ; the guns blazed away. And hundreds of Turks just stood— stood awaiting the bullets or the shrapnel splinters that were going to end their days of war. Then, and only then, I realized to the full the meaning of Eastern fatalism.

'Drome. Sandwiches. Coffee. Maybe a bottle of ale to take back in the plane. Against " regs " but—maybe mail to read while flying back. No need to worry about the Hun Archie or machine-gun fire from the ground. This flying to the butcher's shop had got to be as much a matter of routine as getting the tram or train to work.

Here's the stricken snake again. Only it's quieter now—the coils do not thresh so much. There'll be still less movement when we get this load

off. Ttttt, Tttttt. Crash ! Crash ! Thank God
for a helpful thought——for every one of these poor
devils I kill, there'll be one less to take toll of our
cavalry or infantry when they come up. But, oh,
that nauseating smell of cordite, the pools of blood
we could see, the debris framed by those barren
desolate hills of Samaria.

We were a tough bunch. But we were sickened.
The infantry, hardened warriors that they were,
were absolutely appalled when they came up. They
took a hundred or so prisoners——all that were left.
But there were heaps of smouldering, putrifying
dead. The survivors had tried to dispose of their
dead by burning them. Not because of any relig-
ious rites, but in a desperate effort to protect their
own health. Dead in the East are deadly dangerous
to the living. So these poor few that were still alive
had piled heaps of those who had gone, poured petrol
on them, and lit the rude pyres. The disembowelled
horses and oxen——well, they just didn't matter.
The stench. . . . No, we didn't have to put up with
that. We butchers had the engines and the slip-
streams to protect our dainty nostrils.

When the infantry came up our job was finished.
Thank God for a drink.

In those two days, over what became the Nine
Miles of Dead, our squadron dropped three tons of
bombs and fired 30,000 machine-gun rounds.
We, of No. 1 Squadron, were the chief butchers ;
the Royal Air Force squadrons, between them, only
dropped and fired the same quantity. Six tons of
bombs on targets surrounded by rock, bottom and

NINE MILES OF DEAD

Two views : After the wreckage had been cleared, and the dead removed.

sides—rock that splintered and spurted out missiles as deadly as bullets. Sixty thousand rounds. Targets—average range a hundred feet.

I don't know the extent of the Turkish casualties. I have never been able to find out, and frankly I would rather not know.

While on this subject of enemy casualties, these figures of our squadron may be of interest. In the two months prior to Allenby's ride the squadron accounted for every hostile aircraft shot down on the front. It destroyed seventeen Huns and drove down thirty-three. It carried out 157 strat. recos, seventy-seven photographic recos, and made 150 bomb raids, and dropped 45,948 pounds of bombs.

After the Nine Miles of Dead there were other jobs. We were still the spearhead of the drive. We went east bombing, bombing, bombing. A few days after the annihilation of the Ferweh column, our bombs were falling at Rayak, 120 miles north. The targets were smaller—our land forces had been taking toll—and the fleeing survivors were in smaller formations.

To take the nasty taste of the foregoing out of your mouth, here is the story of another but different and later holocaust—one with our Light Horse in the big rôle. You had to be a Light Horseman fully to appreciate its poignancy.

I was a Light Horseman before Lady Luck sent me to the squadron. I came to know just how much a horse counted. He got you into action; he got you out. He was a friend. No one who was in them will ever forget those long dreary desert stunts

S

after we crossed the canal : Romani, Katia, Oghratina, Bir el Abd, Magdhaba, Rafa. Especially Romani. When the whole Turkish Army attacked the 1st A.L.H. Brigade were holding the line between Mount Meredith and Mount Royston. All night the brigade beat off bayonet charges. Early next morning came the sorely-needed reinforcements, and Jacko's attack was turned into a rout. We chased him—chased him with horses, most of which had been without water for forty hours and more. This was in the desert and in summer.

That does not sound impressive ? No ? Well, try lying out on the beach wearing full service kit, handling a hot rifle, and not otherwise daring to move. The thermometer read 128 degrees in the shade, although God knows where they found shade. Then mount your horse, which already has a little load of 100 pounds, and gallop towards a vicious swirling dust-cloud that covers retreating Turks. No, I shall not forget my mount that night as the fantasses came up with water. He looked at me and, if eyes ever spoke, he said : " I will be pleased when my turn comes." When, as was the case on this occasion, there was neither time nor equipment to water the horses as per " regs," we used to punch in the top of our hats and fill the depression with water from our bottles. Not exactly easy for the horses to get at, but dear old Prince would never spill a drop. And his eyes used to say " Thank you ! " rather than " Isn't there any more ? "

Late the following afternoon three brigades of Light Horse and a Cavalry brigade attacked Bir el

Abd—attacked at the gallop over the soft desert sand.

There was a sight ! Four lines, crescent-shaped, and over four miles long, going hell for leather. I am a movie fan, and like " westerns." But when I hear the people in the theatre getting all hot and bothered when the mob of cowboys are galloping to the rescue, I cannot help thinking : " Yes, that looks he-mannish and all that kind of thing . . . but you never saw the charge at Bir el Abd."

Well, to come to the holocaust. No A.I.F. horses came back to Australia. Only one head—that of Sandy, the charger of the late General Bridges. It is now in the War Museum. I don't know what became of the horses on the Western Front, but I do know what happened to those at our end. Owing to the danger of contagion as regards certain Eastern animal diseases, the horses could not be returned to Australia. One of two choices was open—to sell the horses there, or destroy them. The choice was officially given to the individual Light Horsemen. In the event of the first decision, the horses would be submitted at public auction.

But the troopers knew how the Gyppos treated their mules and donkeys. Would their Australian horses be treated differently ? Especially when it was remembered that the Gyppos did not exactly love the Australian, and that, with one of those queer, mongrel, Eastern aberrations, he might take out his revenge on the horses. No, there could only be one choice. And so the second holocaust happened at the Tripoli Quarry, north of Beirut, where centuries of work had left huge excavations. There, thousands of good soldiers did their bravest act of the war. They killed their dear comrades to save them from an alien, a degraded living. Led the horses to the edge, fired a shot and . . .

It was a terrible thing, that the last shot fired on service should be at a friend who had . . . But you understand. You will know, too, why hundreds of rough, burly Aussies, with useless lead rope or bridle in hand, stumbled blindly away from the edge of the quarry, sobbing their hearts out.

CHAPTER XV

THE BIG PEACE

Whenever all other topics of yarning petered out, there was always one that could be resurrected " over there "—what one would like to do when peace was declared. Each time we did our wishing, a new idea would crop up. A new miscreant was mentally booked for a horrid fate. Or a new job had been thought out: a new thirst or hunger had to be gratified. Lord only knows we had time enough in which to do the wishing. In 1914 we were told that the war could not possibly last more than a few months. As the years rolled on Echo made all kinds of obscene and derisive noises. In the early part of 1918 Peace was not even a " tote bet."

But on 31 October Johnny Turk threw in the towel. Followed a general leave exodus of officers and men from all units, to Cairo, Alexandria, etc. Leave had been piling up for months and, in some cases, for years. So money was plentiful, even without the er——" pickings " of Allenby's ride. Some units had been warned to hold themselves in readiness to move to the Western Front; No. 1 Squadron A.F.C. expected to be rushed off to France at any hour. All of which made Cairo leave the more exciting. And so those officers who were fortunate enough to secure the special fourteen days' leave were well into a fluid stride when news came from England that the Germans were being rolled up in a similar fashion to that which had finished his ally Jacko. Well, most of us had promised ourselves that if ever we were in one peace when Peace came along, the sky would be the limit.

We fellows in the East were fortunate in more ways than one. For when the Armistice (*the* Armistice) came along on 11 November we had had eleven days of celebration of our own Armistice, and were " trained " to the minute to celebrate the major Armistice. We went mad, mad, mad. Mad with joy, relief, emotion. Here was excuse, no, cause— that's the word—cause, for the perfect bender, the colossal binge. It was.

In Cairo, the headquarters of Joy Unlimited was Shepheard's. Here came hundreds, thousands, of officers—admirals, generals, colonels, the whole darn box and dice down to the newest one-pip artists. Rank was forgotten. There in the domain of Black Joe you'd see generals standing drinks to the hitherto less-than-dust lieutenants: jovially, joyously calling on strange juniors to name their poison. You'd see other high and mighty ones having their backs pounded by small Navy, Army, or Air Force fry— and liking it. But since he plays such an important part in the Joy Unconfined I must introduce you to Black Joe.

Joe was the O.C. of Shepheard's cocktail bar. Well over six feet in height, big cheery face, apparently hundreds, thousands of pearly white teeth always on show. Immaculate whites, and a red sash and tarboush. He knew every cocktail that ever was and a lot that were to be. Yes, he was the High Priest of Cocktaildom, and he looked the part. The " horse's neck " was one of his specials. When this was followed, as a chaser, by a " broken spur," the cumulative effect was as if the whole world was washed with golden, caressing fire and happy, friendly glory. Only a brace of Galle Face gin-slings could achieve the same effect on me.

Between the Armistices—that word brings to mind a bright thought—how would armistices go as a test word in under-the-influence interrogations ? But I'm getting off my course. What I set out to say was that in the dual-armistice celebration, I was normal only in the fact that I was as subnormal or abnormal as the rest of us.

Them's were the days ! Black Joe was always busy, but on 11 November he must have been the busiest man in the East. There was a struggling mass of uniformed humanity ten to fifteen deep about the bar. Joe never lost his smile, even when it had a minor waterfall splashing down it. How that chap perspired ! But his assistants looked as if the strain was too heavy to be borne.

Of course we were all drunk, many times drunk. Army, Navy, and Air Force ; we had fought our war and we had won. That was that. This was Peace, and there was enough money in Shepheard's to pay for our celebration.

Only miracle men could stand up to this pro-digious eleven-day bender. Being no miracle man, I was reclining in the *patio*, suffering a recovery, when I saw what might be called a typical celebration scene. A *gharry*, drawn by two horses and driven by a Gyppo from the usual box-seat, was moving quietly along the street when about twenty Light Horsemen (not so quiet) pulled it up. I could not hear the conversation, but apparently the upshot was not to the taste of the Aussies. Abdul was pulled down from his seat, two of the Aussies mounted the horses, three clambered on to the driver's box, while about ten more wedged themselves into the passenger section.

But what is that non-passenger doing with that gadget? Looks like a wrench of sorts. As the *gharry* moves off, the non-passenger trots alongside one of the back wheels. He is doing something we cannot see from the *patio*. A pal and I are curious. We pull ourselves together and amble down the street to have a look-see. We get to the scene in time to see the villain at work. Yes, it is a wrench he has, and it is clamped on the rear axle-nut. The nut comes off, but the wheel refuses to follow. The horses, because of their unusual load, are just down to a walk. Stern measures now. The villain doubles to the rear of the *gharry*, and, with an " issue " daisy-crusher, gives the turning wheel a furious kick. That does it. Off comes the wheel. Crash! Diggers, *gharry*, and horses tangle up in a glorious ruin.

Laughing made me thirsty. Back to Shepheard's and Black Joe. Things were getting boisterous. Inter-service arguments were under way. The Battle of Jutland and the retreat from Mons were under review by vinous critics, and a lot of haloes were the worse for wear. Toasts in between, all the time. Then suddenly someone would shout above the babel : " Gentlemen, the King! " Instant silence. Then : " The King—God bless him! " Depending on your viewpoint, it was extraordinary, or it wasn't, how meticulously the toast was observed. Remember though, you sceptics, that we were in uniform. Dinner that night was a memory-and-a-half. Food! Who wanted food ? We optimists could exist until to-morrow. We wanted music and song and more song. Yes, and drink. There were over five hundred of us jammed at the dining-tables, and the Gyppo waiter certainly knew there was a Peace on. " Bring some wine iggrey imshi, yaller ! " They brought. Kept on bringing.

Towards midnight the grand finale got under way —in the great annexe of the hotel. This was an enormous room, furnished in keeping with a hotel in the world class. Pictures, tapestries, bric-à-brac would have adorned the mansion of an art connoisseur. And there was a wonderful red carpet. It had quantity as well as quality. It was about six feet wide and it ran the full length of the annexe, out past the hotel shops, past the offices and out to the inside entrance to the *patio*. It was hundreds of feet long, and all in one piece. It was the chief ornament of a hotel famous for its ornaments.

Well, towards midnight, the pickled mass in the annexe—I'd love to have Black Joe's takings that day—were ripe for a collective mischief. Suddenly a high-pitched Oxford-model voice, slightly the worse for alcoholic wear, rang across the room :

" Come on, Army and Navy! Let's take on the Air Force."

We were slightly outnumbered, but Army and Navy were aged and slightly musty. This was a challenge.

" Flying Corps, rally! " roared a major, a squadron commander, just as if he were waggling his joystick and rallying his formation to attack. There were no rules. But, by general assent, the resultant battle was a matter of scrums, each side heaving to push the other over. Unfortunately furniture had not been warned to keep off the arena and its attitude of passive neutrality was no protection. Pictures, tapestries, mirrors, bric-à-brac, light fittings, windows, all became casualties. There were human casualties too, but there were only those due to the earlier doings with Bacchus. There were rough-and-tumbles and horseplay aplenty, but no tough stuff. We were like a mob of young puppies, full of frolic and fun. But I have to grin now, at the thought of admirals, generals, and wing commanders bucking into a scrum and joining in " sacks on the mill."

Well, things had reached the stage when it seemed as if the walls might strike a spot of bother, when a stentorian and authoritative voice boomed " Stop " What's going on here ? " Stop we did, and after disentangling ourselves, we looked toward the "stop" source. Oho! No one else than the A.P.M. and he, even among Jacks, notorious. He was a bully, an over-zealous crime-seeker. Also he was an " intruder." After a moment's silence, and while the A.P.M. looked all kinds of terrible things, a voice

roared from what had been the second row of an
Army scrum:

" Tackle him low, troops, and roll the ——— out of
the place! "

An excellent idea. The A.P.M. went down
under a sea of khaki, blue, and grey. As, amidst
cheers and jeers, he was being dragged towards the
exit, someone had a brain-wave. Then the A.P.M.
was dumped on the end of the giant carpet and was
rolled in it. By the time it approached the *patio*,
the roll was of huge proportions and a hefty crowd
was necessary to move it. But out it went, through
the main entrance doors, across the *patio*, and then,
with some hearty kicks, was sent, bumpety-bumpety-
bump, down the steps leading into the Sharia Nubar
Pasha. It rolled across the pavement and on to the
street. Crowds of us watched it stopped by excited
Gyppos: and enjoyed the strenuous efforts made by
the A.P.M. to extricate himself from his cocoon.
We cheered him as he left. That was one of the
finest victories of the Peace.

But the hotel management did not think so when
they surveyed the now-deserted battle area. But
this was one time at least when roystering service
men had a thought to the morrow. I don't know
where it all came from, but a big sum was handed to
the management next day. It was a peace offering.
. . . For the best " Peace " I ever had.

EPILOGUE

Now, looking back, it does seem as if one of the greatest tasks of the war was the change over from war to peace. Actually we did not think of it at all until the job was done; there were too many other exciting things. But take just one phase: What became of all the stupendous supplies ? But maybe that is an unpleasant subject—it leads to the pocket; and we are still paying for the solution of that problem.

I can, at all events, tell you how our squadron broke up. It was a big job. Although we were only a tiny unit—260 officers and men—we had a lot of gear. Aeroplanes, workshops, wireless gear, hangars, huge stores, and our own self-contained moving outfit of thirty lorries and cars. The aircraft, of course, were flown in the moving operations. Well, one day there came the long-awaited order from Wing : " No. 1 Squadron, A.F.C., will transfer all equipment on charge to No. 111 Squadron, R.A.F., Ramleh." That simplified things. No need for us to have the bother and the headache of stowing away our gear in the British war cupboard. So we flew, drove, or were otherwise transported, lock, stock, and barrel, to Ramleh. There the Tommy squadron was headed by Major Hereward de Havilland—since better known as " D.H." to every worth-while civil and service pilot in Australia.

So far as we pilots were concerned, the hand-over was not as easy as we imagined it was going to be. Those machines had come to mean something very important to us. After all, we were still alive and well ; but if those buses had not been as good as they were, would we have been handing over ? Those old Bristols had done their part. Now they were going out of our hands, out of our lives to strangers who didn't know, and probably didn't care. It was a big wrench. Just before the last parade, a lot of us casually—at least we tried to make it look that way—strolled into the hangars to look a last good-bye. Some of the lads souvenired the registration markings on the fin. And I'll swear that some of them, as they patted the prop, said something that only the planes heard and understood.

The final dinner of our squadron was an over-powering affair. Oceans of grog and great junket-ings. Lots of our pals in the other squadrons and units had been, or were, there to say good-bye. There was Medhurst from No. 14, the only Eng-lishman to command the squadron—that was when our C.O. had a spot of leave. Very much a man, that chap. And Dan Deakin, Sheppard, and Grebby from No. 111 ; " Mo " Morrison, Cloggy, Toc C. Macauley, and Gower from Wing ; and Lord only knows how many more. To the Tommy visitors, our pals, there was a general and an indivi-dual invitation :

" Come out to Aussie and look us up. You'll have a great time—we'll see to that."

Early next morning, the last parade. Officers and men had only their personal kit. It was all so brief and simple. One minute we were a squadron, a champion squadron. Then :

" Fall in ! " " Shun ! " " Squadron will advance in columns of fours, H.Q. flight leading. Qu-u-u-ick march ! "

We marched away to the railway station, but, as we passed the hangars, many a head turned for a last look. There was the nose of a Bristol looking out of each. I wonder if those three buses passed the word back to the others. I wonder if they said: " They're gone."

It was the only train trip the squadron had had. Twelve hours by the clock, but as we passed through Medjel, Belah, Bir el Abd, and Romani, and remembered our squadron dead there, the train trip detoured into the past.

Kantara, and awaiting embarkation. No war, no machines, no parades. Things got dull. When were we going to get out of this stinking hole ? Oh yes, there was one bright thing. During the final stage of Allenby's offensive some of the abandoned German staff cars strayed into squadron hands. They were wonderful jobs, brothers and sisters of those we used to chase along the Jenin road. They grew so attached to us that they refused to leave. They were supposed to be handed over to No. 111 with the other gear. When they jibbed at the transfer, we shooed them away. And—would you believe it—when we reached Kantara, there were the faithful beasts awaiting us! Of course, such touching devotion had to be rewarded. We took them for long rides to Port Said, Ismailia, Cairo. We gave 'em lots of bright company. And then, at the finish, they were so heartbroken at the prospect of being without us, that we couldn't leave them in un-Australian hands. . . . So we drove 'em into the sea.

One day, towards the end, an Australian pilot walked into Major de Havilland's office. He had come 180 miles from Kantara by train. He would like, he said to the major, to have a last flip in his old bus.

" Not on your blanky life," snorted D.H. " If I were fool enough to let you get off the ground in her, the next I would hear about it would be from the president of a Field General Court Martial, asking me to explain how one of the machines of my squadron had mysteriously appeared in Australia. No, sir! You fellows would souvenir the Pyramids if you could find some mug to buy 'em."

" Don't be hard, sir, you can trust me. I'll bring her back O.K., and if you feel like it, what about coming up in the back seat ? "

" No thanks. I got through this war with a whole skin and I don't intend to subject myself to the last flight of a sentimental Aussie. Take a pull at yourself, me lad."

The interview became prolonged, and at last the pleadings of the Aussie won the day. But he was only allowed the farewell flip on the understanding that, not as an individual, but as a representative of No. 1 Squadron, A.F.C., he would take farewell of the Bristols, per 4626.

There was a nice touch in that sentimental pilgrimage. The pilot picked a handful of Palestine poppies. And when old 4626 circled over Ramleh cemetery, the poppies fluttered down. Below, sleeping the good soldier's sleep, lay Wally Farquhar, Hal Letch, Johnny Walker, Ernie Stooke, Bob Craig, Curwen-Walker, Fell and Jensen, all old squadron comrades.

This book is my poppies.